D1009794

AMERICAN HIGHER EDUCATION IN CRISIS?

WHAT EVERYONE NEEDS TO KNOW®

AMERICAN HIGHER EDUCATION IN CRISIS?

WHAT EVERYONE NEEDS TO KNOW®

GOLDIE BLUMENSTYK

OXFORD
UNIVERSITY PRESS

OXFORD

UNIVERSITY PRESS

Oxford University Press is a department of the University of Oxford.
It furthers the University's objective of excellence in research, scholarship,
and education by publishing worldwide.

Oxford   New York
Auckland   Cape Town   Dar es Salaam   Hong Kong   Karachi
Kuala Lumpur   Madrid   Melbourne   Mexico City   Nairobi
New Delhi   Shanghai   Taipei   Toronto

With offices in
Argentina   Austria   Brazil   Chile   Czech Republic   France   Greece
Guatemala   Hungary   Italy   Japan   Poland   Portugal   Singapore
South Korea   Switzerland   Thailand   Turkey   Ukraine   Vietnam

Oxford is a registered trademark of Oxford University Press
in the UK and certain other countries.

"What Everyone Needs to Know" is a registered trademark of
Oxford University Press.

Published in the United States of America by
Oxford University Press
198 Madison Avenue, New York, NY 10016

Library of Congress Cataloging-in-Publication Data
Blumenstyk, Goldie.
American higher education in crisis? : what everyone needs
to know / Goldie Blumenstyk.
pages cm. — (What everyone needs to know)
Includes bibliographical references and index.
ISBN 978-0-19-937408-3 (paperback)—ISBN 978-0-19-937409-0 (cloth)
1. Education, Higher—United States.   2. Universities and colleges
United States. 3. Education, Higher—Aims and objectives—United States.   I. Title.
LA227.4.B59 2014
378.00973—dc23
2014016159

1 3 5 7 9 8 6 4 2
Printed in the United States of America
on acid-free paper

CONTENTS

PART THREE: WHO'S IN CHARGE? LEADERSHIP PRESSURES—FROM WITHIN AND WITHOUT   99

PART FOUR: WHAT'S AHEAD   125

FACTS AND FIGURES ON AMERICAN HIGHER EDUCATION

Enrollment by type of institution, Fall, 2013

Total Enrollment, all sectors	19,885, 203	
Four-year public	7,796,119	39.2 percent
Two-year public	6,497,602	32.6 percent
Four-year private nonprofit	3,761,953	18.9 percent
Four-year for-profit	1,321,107	6.6 percent

(Source: National Student Clearinghouse Research Center)

Total enrollment includes the estimated 2 percent of students enrolled at the same time at more than one institution. Many for-profit colleges do not participate with the Clearinghouse so the totals for that sector and overall enrollment may actually be greater than estimated. Percentages do not add up to 100 because figures for students enrolled in less-than-two-year institutions, as well as those at private and for-profit two-year colleges, are not listed separately but are included in the total. Between fall 2011 and fall 2013, enrollments at four-year for-profit colleges fell by 22.1 percent and at two-year public colleges by 6 percent.

Average Published Charges for Full-Time Undergraduates, by Type and Control of Institution, 2013–14

Public two-year, in-state	$3,264
Public four-year, in state	$8,893
Public four-year, out-of-state	$22,203
Private nonprofit four-year	$30,094
For-profit	$15,130

(Source: "Trends in College Pricing, 2013" The College Board)

Enrollment of Students With Pell Grants, by Institution Type, 2011–12

Public two-year colleges:	3.4 million Pell Grant recipients
Public four-year colleges:	2.8 million Pell Grant recipients
For-profit colleges:	2.1 million Pell Grant recipients
Private nonprofit colleges:	1.2 million Pell Grant recipients

(Source: September 2013 Congressional Budget Office report on Pell Grants)

Pell Grant recipients made up a larger share of the student body—63 percent—at for-profit colleges than at other types in 2011–2012. Public two-year colleges had the smallest proportion of recipients among their students, 32 percent, compared with 35 percent at public four-year colleges and 37 percent at private nonprofits.

AUTHOR'S NOTE

I walked into the Northeast Washington, D.C., community center just as the twenty high-school students upstairs began digging into their pizza. The students, some of them from other poor neighborhoods a Metro ride away, had made their way on this bitter-cold night to attend their weekly sessions with mentors in a local program called College Bound, a nonprofit organization that works to help public-school kids in the D.C. area prepare for and succeed in college. It was the start of a two-day period in January 2014 that, in many ways, encapsulated for me some of the challenges and opportunities higher education now faces—as well as the enormous stakes for society.

I came to observe the session after hearing about the program from a college friend of mine who volunteers as a mentor at a different College Bound site. I've interviewed hundreds of students as a reporter and editor at *The Chronicle of Higher Education*, but as I immersed myself in the writing of this book, I thought it would be useful to again hear directly from young people about their college hopes and expectations. I talked first with Moses Kennedy, an eighteen-year-old track star at McKinley Tech High School with a strong B average, who participated regularly in the program. Moses's younger brother, Elihu, was working with his mentor at the next folding table. Their mother is a secretary at NASA, and their father works for Amtrak, cleaning trains. Their three older siblings had gone to college, and Moses, with one scholarship offer from Clark Atlanta University already in hand and hopes for others, had decided in no uncertain terms that he would be going, too, hoping to study computer science or athletic training. "What I've been told is it limits your opportunity if you don't go to college," he said, matter-of-factly.

In more-affluent neighborhoods, Moses's ambitions to attend college would hardly stand out. In the United States today, a person from an upper-income family is nearly nine times more likely to have earned a bachelor's degree by age twenty-four than is one from a poor family.[1] And with globalization, the decline of good-paying manufacturing jobs, and other changes, the long-term economic and social risks of not having a college degree, or at least some education beyond high school, grow ever greater.

Moses and the other teenagers at the community center that night, all black, all needing substantial amounts of financial aid to get them to college, have gotten that message. It is the reason they return each week, honing their essay-writing skills, practicing math exercises, and working through their inhibitions to polish their public speaking. The odds may be against them, but their goals are clear. With a college education, said Kyra Gilkes, who was dreaming of attending Spelman College, "I can give my family a better life." And without such an education, said her friend Imani Hooper, who is aiming for a career in medicine after attending Spelman or perhaps Ohio State University, "I would just feel like a failure." Imani said she was all too aware of the "statistics and the stereotypes" about black people lacking a college education and getting stuck in a cycle of poverty, and she was not about to become part of that.

The aspirations of those students—to go to college, on a traditional campus, the way I myself had over three decades ago—were still fresh the next morning while I sat at my computer and began poking through the videos and assigned readings of one of the new experiments in higher education. It was a tuition-free online course from Duke University, served up with an assist from a venture-capital-backed company called Coursera. The class: the "History and Future of (Mostly) Higher Education." My classmates: 18,000-plus people across six continents. We had all signed up for a new kind of educational offering known as a MOOC—a massive open online course. Our professor, Cathy Davidson, pitched it as more than a typical college course; it was also one piece of the larger alternative-education movement now working to re-shape the very nature of higher education.

That night, about a mile from where the teenagers had told me of their college hopes the previous evening, President Obama stood before Congress to deliver his State of the Union address. He eschewed the harsher rhetoric he has frequently used to lambast colleges about rising costs and poor value, but nonetheless made clear that "shaking up our system of higher education" was still high on his administration's agenda, as was doing more to help students and families "who feel trapped by student loan debt."

College costs and student debt; public reproach that extends all the way to the White House; disruptive innovations in teaching that challenge traditional modes and mores of college; the vital need for the educational opportunities made possible by college, particularly for those striving for a foothold in the middle class: When I set out with this book to capture the essentials of today's higher education crisis—certainly the gravest and most exciting that I have seen in my twenty-six-plus years of higher-education reporting—I knew that each of those themes would be a crucial piece of this evolving story. The reminder that very real people with very real dreams depend on how these and a host of other challenges are resolved was a constant motivation to me as I stepped back from day-to-day journalism to make sense of the complex forces of change now unfolding in higher education.

But first: a little truth-in-advertising. While in the pages that follow I have sought to provide the basics of "what everyone needs to know" to understand America's higher education crisis, these chapters by no means cover all aspects of the myriad issues colleges face today. I have written nothing about the crisis in science funding threatening the future of young academic scientists or the gloomy job prospects for the glut of PhD holders graduating each year from research universities, nothing about the concerns over sexual assaults, binge drinking, and other "campus-climate" issues, precious little about the academic scandals that continue to plague college athletics, and have no doubt altogether skipped other matters that some may consider grave omissions.

It is difficult to write in generalities about American higher education because it is not homogeneous. The United States does not have a higher-education system; in effect it has dozens of them. It is not only the case that the different tacks that states take toward higher education, for example, can have a huge impact on the character and finances of colleges (even private ones); colleges are also bound—and, frankly, compete—based on their differing missions, traditions, and institutional character. An institution like Maryland's Harford Community College no doubt has a lot more in common with community colleges in other states than it does with the University of Maryland at College Park, the state's flagship university. Small Catholic colleges may identify more with small Lutheran institutions than with the University of Notre Dame. And what may be a challenge for a comprehensive four-year university in Illinois that draws students from its local region is not necessarily a problem for a selective New England private college attracting applicants from a national pool, or for a private research university with a vast medical enterprise and international collaborations around the globe. Not all of the issues described in this book apply evenly, or even at all, across the board. But I have tried to focus on those with the broadest effect.

As for the impact of that movement Professor Davidson was hoping to galvanize with her Duke course: Don't ask me. I dropped out after the first week. I'm told it was an interesting course, but with no real grades or money on the line, it was one experimental educational experience I could afford to skip. Millions of people have signed up for MOOCs in the past few years and most, like me, never finish them. There may be a small lesson in that, too. Colleges face mounting pressures to do more with less. Until about a year ago, many pundits were proclaiming the potential for mass education through the MOOC model as one potential answer to that challenge, just as pundits had earlier declared the virtual-reality experiments of Second Life (remember that?) the future of teaching, and as some are now exuberantly touting competency-based education as the next great answer to higher-education's cost and quality conundrum. Innovations in higher education can be exciting, but the luster often fades as reality sets in.

Like others with long experience in this field, I'm often asked what's next for higher education. How much more expensive can it get? If not MOOCs, is there another innovation—data-driven personalized education, perhaps—that will radically change the experience? Frankly, it's impossible to say with certainty how higher education will change, and one should have serious doubts about anyone who says they know. It is safe to say, however, that there is no one "killer app," but rather a combination of many of these ideas that will inform the future.

What is certain is that the pressures are real, the need for colleges to innovate is pressing, and the changes, some of them already underway, will be myriad. And it is vital to recognize that the risks in getting in it wrong, in rushing headlong toward the next shiny thing without careful consideration of what, and more importantly, who, will be left behind, are all too great. It's in that spirit that I offer what I hope will be a useful grounding in some of the most crucial developments and issues of this next era of higher-education evolution.

INTRODUCTION

Is higher education in America in crisis?

Over the past thirty years, the price of college has gone up faster than prices of almost all other goods and services. Student debt is at an all-time high of $1.2 trillion. Doubts about the value of college are on the rise. State support for the public-college sector, which educates seven of ten students, has yet to (and may never) return to the generous levels of the early 2000s. The financial model underlying many private colleges is becoming more and more fragile. Collectively, colleges reflect—some say even amplify—the racial and income inequities of the nation's neighborhoods and elementary and secondary schools. Demands for career-focused training are growing, even as experts argue that the skills of a liberal arts education are becoming increasingly important. And a restless reform movement, inspired by the promise of new technology and backed by powerful political and financial might, is growing more insistent that the enterprise spend less, show better results, and become more open to new kinds of educational providers.

So in a word, Yes. Higher education is most assuredly in crisis.

Does that spell doom for the thousands of colleges that make up American higher education? Does it mean a death knell for the country's multitude of institutions—public and private, religious and secular, older and younger, large and small, urban and rural, well-endowed and struggling, research-intensive giants and humanities-focused bantams, for-profit and not, all-online and determinedly residential, historically black and adult-market focused?

It certainly does not.

Anyone who has read a newspaper or magazine in the last three or four years, listened to the news, checked out a local bookstore, or even stumbled into a film festival has no doubt seen or heard a different conclusion. The doomsday narrative is seemingly everywhere, with predictions of a massive "shake-out" coming to the postsecondary-education landscape because of rising costs and recession-weakened finances, and of a "college bubble" on the verge of bursting under the crushing weight of student debt.

But simplistic predictions along those lines fail to recognize the complexity, resources, diversity, and resilience of a sector of society that now educates nearly twenty million undergraduate and graduate students a year.[1] The predictions ignore the impact that the ebb and flow of economic cycles have always had on colleges, cycles like the ones that prompted alarmist reports about the financial viability of more than half of all colleges at the tail end of the 1960s, and the college-bubble anxieties of the mid 1970s that led to Richard Barry Freeman's *The Overeducated American*.[2] For the thirty years that followed the publication of that book, enrollments boomed and most colleges flourished.

Today's dire predictions also overlook the adaptations many colleges have already undertaken. Witness, for instance, the growing use of data analytics by colleges to help students stay on track toward their degrees, the incorporation of technologies that allow for greater personalization in pedagogy, the increasing number of community colleges where students can now earn a more-affordable bachelor's degree, and the more than five million students now taking classes online or in "hybrid" formats that mix distance education with face-to-face instruction.

Still, nearly four centuries since a band of forward-thinking Puritan ministers in 1636 founded America's first college—later to be called Harvard—to train clergy for their new colony, it is clear that today's ferment over costs, value, and efficacy is leaving no college untouched.

This is not an unprecedented phenomenon. Economic, political, demographic, religious, and technological forces have transformed higher education before. They are what brought forth public land-grant universities under the Morrill Act of 1862; the first wave of higher-education democratization via the GI Bill after World War II; the spread of community colleges after 1965; the expansion of the federal student-loan system in 1992; and the emergence of the modern for-profit-college industry in the late 1990s as the Internet (and a loosening of federal student-aid regulations) opened the door to distance education.

Now higher education as an enterprise is once again at a watershed. Or more accurately, it is in the thick of the currents. The disquiet around higher education runs deep and wide: its price, its quality, its responsiveness to changing conditions and new populations. But ultimately, it begins with the question that echoes in those doomsday narratives: Is postsecondary education still worth it?

That is a question that is itself freighted with complexities. In the past, higher education has always been seen as both a public and a private good. But over the past few decades, college leaders and policy makers have increasingly touted the financial payoff from a college degree as an individual benefit (in part to justify rising prices), and individual and collective expectations of college have changed. Society does still benefit from a more-educated populace—college graduates are healthier, vote at higher rates, pay more in taxes, are more likely to read literature, volunteer at higher rates, and are even more likely to wear seat belts.[3] But that is not often what drives the national conversation on higher education. Instead, it centers primarily on the economic imperatives of the twenty-first century, and the expectation that colleges will produce the graduates to help fill those demands. By 2020, according to experts, two-thirds of all jobs will require at least some education and training beyond high school (versus 28 percent of jobs forty years ago).[4]

The public hears that. As polls by Gallup show, two-thirds of Americans now say a very important reason for getting an education beyond high school is "to get a good job," and separate surveys of college freshmen at four-year colleges find that 88 percent of them say the same. Students may welcome the intellectual growth and broadening experiences that a college education can provide, but since 2006 most have been saying that's not the top reason they are going. More than ever, a college education is seen less as a process and more as a product, a means to an end. And customers are not entirely convinced that what they are buying is worth the price.

With the rationale for college turning more and more on salaries and labor-market payoffs, college leaders and faculty members at all but the most career-focused of colleges are uncomfortable as well. Many inside those institutions—as well as many without—now worry that the higher-minded aspects of higher education—to nurture students' social, cultural, and intellectual growth and help them to develop into not just twenty-first century workers but also citizens of a twenty-first century world—are being diminished if not altogether lost.

The emphasis has shifted from the importance to society of a well-rounded, college-educated populace to the personal gains of attending college. But does college even provide those highly touted individual benefits? The projections on future employment trends, coupled with years of evidence of the economic return of a college degree, give most observers the confidence to say that college still pays financially. But more than ever there is a nuanced calculus that underlies that assertion. Where did you attend? How much did you have to pay or borrow? Where were you hired when you graduated? They all play into the equation. As the college-cost scholar Sandy Baum has put it, "it's not as simple as saying: College pays off." A degree, she notes, "is not a guarantee."

Studies by the Georgetown University Center on Education and the Workforce and organizations like College Measures have recently reinforced this thinking, noting that degrees in particular fields (food sciences and business economics, for example) generally have more economic value than those in others (family and consumer sciences and accounting), even if they seem similar. Studies have also shown that for some people, an associate degree and even a certificate—a credential that is short of a degree—might make better economic sense than a bachelor's degree. Indeed, the Georgetown Center's analysis of U.S. Census data shows that typical workers with associate degrees out-earn 28 percent of those with bachelor's degrees.[5] And in select fields like computing and information services, people with low-cost certificates likewise can often make more than those with bachelor's degrees.[6]

Yet broadly speaking, the payoffs of a traditional college education are undeniable. Median earnings for bachelor's degree holders are 65 percent greater than for those with just a high-school diploma over a 40-year working career, according to the latest data from the College Board. Those with associate degrees, typically earned at community and technical colleges, make 27 percent more.[7] College-educated workers also fared far better than those with only a high-school education as the economy was shedding jobs during the economic crash that began in 2008. And the unemployment rate for people with a college degree is now still about half of what it is for those with only a high-school diploma.[8] It's not so much that a college degree adds to people's wages; rather, it offers more protection from the financial perils of the modern economy compared with a high-school education. Poverty rates for young people with only a high school diploma are three times higher today, for example, than they were in 1979 when the baby boomers were young. [9]

Still, doubt about the value of a degree reigns, some of it fueled by the phenomenon of underemployment of recent college graduates. Studies suggest that more than a third of them are now "mal-employed"—holding jobs that do not require a degree. Yet that may be less a problem of over-education than a symptom of the broader sluggish economy and a mismatch in skills. Nearly half of all entry-level jobs requiring a bachelor's degree are in science, technology, engineering, and mathematics fields, according to an analysis of job postings by a company called Burning Glass, but only about 29 percent of undergraduates earn degrees in a STEM field.[10] Additionally, in the past, according to the College Board, to the extent that there was an underemployment problem, it was almost always a temporary one. Based on that, the organization says even today, college is worth the price. An eighteen-year-old who graduates college in four years can expect to "break even" on the costs of being out of the workforce and borrowing the full cost of the average college tuition and fees by age thirty-six, according to the College Board's calculations—and if they attend a public college, four years sooner than that, based on the lower average tuition and fees.[11]

But all of these projections are based on historical patterns, which may not take into account the longer time it takes for many students to earn a degree, the hard truths of the current economy, or, as Andrew P. Kelly of the American Enterprise Institute's Center on Higher Education puts it, the challenges that "overpriced colleges and universities" face today as they begin to confront increasing competition from alternative-education providers who are appearing on the higher-education landscape. "Colleges are still clinging to their traditional credentialing monopoly," Kelly says, but for some of them, that may be a more fragile lifeline than they realize.[12]

The simple fact is that cost structures—and prices—of colleges have grown much faster than the public's ability to pay for them. In the early 1980s, the average sticker price for a private college equaled about 20 percent of the median annual family income, and that of a public college about 5 percent. By 2002, the average sticker price of a private college equaled 40 percent of the median family income and a public college would have taken up nearly 10 percent. But rising prices combined with stagnating incomes makes for a painful mix. In 2012, with the median family income about 10-percent below its all-time 1999 high, the average sticker price for a private college climbed to a level equal to a staggering 55 percent of the median family income. Even the sticker price of a public college would have required more than 16 percent of the median household income.[13]

Most students do not pay those full sticker prices, thanks to government financial aid and scholarships from colleges based on students' financial need and other criteria. But try explaining that byzantine—and often-unsustainable— discount-based business model to students and their families. And even with this system, the discounts and aid are not always enough. In fall 2013, nearly half of all the first-year students surveyed by researchers at the University of California at Los Angeles for the annual Freshman Survey said cost factors were "very important" in their decision to enroll where they did, up from 15 percent in 2004. Four out of ten students who were accepted to their first choice college but declined to enroll there said they turned it down because they could not afford it.[14]

No wonder the prospect of paying for college—now so vital to economic and social well-being—leaves many middle-class families confused, anxious, and daunted, and those from truly poor households even more discouraged.

College costs are probably the biggest reason for the public concern, but they're not the only ones. For starters, there are the growing doubts about quality of education—are students even learning? That is a question that has gained currency since researchers Richard Arum and Josipa Roska began reporting that too many students failed to improve their writing and reasoning skills while in college. The researchers, authors of the 2011 book *Academically Adrift: Limited Learning on College Campuses* and a follow-up study, based their findings on test results of 2300 students at twenty-four institutions evaluated at the beginning, middle, and end of their college careers, which indicated that more than a third of them showed no statistically significant improvement in their scores on the essay test.

Subsequent analyses by others have found the problem is not as dire as Arum and Roska suggest. Even so, the conclusions in *Academically Adrift*, coupled with studies showing that college students today study fewer hours than their predecessors and that grade-inflation is on the rise (with A's accounting for 43 percent of all grades today, versus 31 percent in 1988 and 15 percent in 1960),[15] have left many to wonder about higher education's rigor and standards. Certainly, it is a concern for employers, who in survey after survey say recent college graduates are not qualified for positions or lack basic workplace skills like the ability to communicate, solve complex problems, or adapt.[16]

For all the discussion in the past few years about improving college-completion rates, graduation-rate trends, too, offer little comfort. On average they've pretty much hovered at a rate just below 60 percent for a decade, according to the U.S. Department of Education's official graduation rate—although this captures only students who have enrolled full-time in college for the first time and then complete their degree at that institution within 150 percent of the expected time. (For a bachelor's degree, that would be six years to complete what has long been considered a "four-year" degree.) Worse yet, according to critics like Mark S. Schneider, a former U.S. commissioner of education statistics, are the dozens of "failure factories," some of them public colleges, where graduation rates of 30 percent or lower continued to decline over the past ten years without any apparent recriminations from their accreditors or other gate-keeping bodies.[17]

Beyond academics, with the money chase in big-time college athletics, revelations about colleges falsifying rankings data, and CEO-style salaries for presidents, colleges have done themselves no favors in recent years when it comes to public perception. Reported abuses by for-profit colleges that aggressively recruit students have added tarnish as well. Little wonder, then, that the mistrust has also given rise to new demands for accountability, reflected most visibly in President Obama's recent push to create a rating system for colleges, and in legislatures, where more than twenty states now tie at least some portion of public funding directly to colleges' performance, even as they provide less and less of the funding.

As we will see, states' disinvestment in higher education is the major cause of the steep rise in tuition prices at public colleges in recent years—sticker prices increased by 80 percent, after inflation, at four-year colleges between 2001 and 2013. But those reductions are part of a broader and longer-term trend that began in the early 1980s, a sign of a country "consuming its future," according to one analyst, Thomas G. Mortenson, of the Pell Institute for the Study of Opportunity in Higher Education. A generation that enjoyed the benefits of low tuition made possible by higher levels of state funding, says Mortenson, is now turning its back on the generations that come after.[18]

Yet state cuts are not the only cause for rising prices at public colleges, and they're not the reason average published tuition at private colleges increased by more than 30 percent since 2001. Colleges are creatures of ambition and competition. But those traits are two-edged swords; they can drive advances in scholarship and quality, but also the misguided practices that produce the "climbing-wall wars" (the name for the race to build the better fitness center) and other spending that adds to colleges' costs and debt loads. And those traits are the reason for the growing use of "presidential scholarships" and similar forms of student aid that are effectively discounts, paid for out of tuition revenues.

Meanwhile, for all the billions of dollars government does still put toward institutions and student aid, higher education is failing as force for social mobility. While access to college is broader than ever, higher education is more stratified by income and race than it has been in two generations, as we discuss in the questions that follow. For-profit colleges and community colleges enroll a disproportionately high number of minority and needy students, while the wealthiest public and private four-year institutions enroll the biggest share of upper-income students. Not only do these inequities matter now, they are a harbinger of the even bigger challenges ahead, as America's college population is predicted to become poorer, older, and more dominated by racial and ethnic minorities (who in fact will soon collectively make up the majority).

That these demographic shifts are occurring as the forces that influence higher education are in flux only adds to the complexity. Faculty power has diminished (due in part to colleges' shift from tenured and tenure-track faculty to adjuncts), while the clout of reform-minded foundations and think tanks pushing policies that are more welcoming to alternative-education models is on the rise, as is the influence of businesses with a direct stake in higher education.

What's at risk? While it's premature to say that colleges' monopoly on credentialing is crumbling, clearly the financial and technological forces now sweeping higher education will leave, or already have left, many more institutions vulnerable.

Consider just one. The impact from the entrée of alternative credit-bearing MOOCs, and of companies like StraighterLine, which with its partner colleges offers dozens of courses at bargain-basement prices, and of organizations like the Saylor Foundation, which makes its courses available for free, could signal difficulty for colleges that are already on shaky financial ground. Many colleges rely on the "profits" they make from general education courses to subsidize other operations. As these alternatives catch on, this "unbundling" of the college mission will have financial consequences.

The chapters that follow will explore these ramifications and many others, unpacking some of the myths and facts about things like the impact of tenure on college costs; providing a picture of the student loan problem that fleshes out the nuances behind student debt; and documenting the hurdles that arise for students from disadvantaged families and inadequate schools. And with "faster and cheaper" (and in some cases, "more profitable") now driving many of the efforts to reinvent higher education, the chapters will also take on the question, "Reinvention for Whom?" as they highlight the power shifts and new forces that have already begun to reshape the way America's students go to college.

Part One

STUDENTS

Who goes to college in America?

The population of the United States is far better educated today than it has ever been, and by some measures, that's a national success story. In 1971, only 12 percent of adults aged twenty-five years and older held a bachelor's degree or higher. By 2012, that proportion had increased to 31 percent. (An additional 10 percent held an associate degree.) During that same period, the percentage of adults who had finished at least some college increased from 22 to 57 percent. The pipeline to college is also expanding, as rates of high-school completion have been rising; between 1971 and 2012, the proportion of the U.S. adult population who had completed high school increased from 57 to 88 percent.[1]

While these gains are notable, they have also been uneven across income levels, racial and ethnic lines, and sexes, and according to several experts, those inequities have been increasing. America has become a more diverse society, but higher-education attainment has not kept pace.

Nearly twenty million people now attend college in the United States—more than sixteen million of them undergraduates and the rest pursuing advanced degrees. In popular culture, the "typical college student" is a young person who enrolls right out of high school at a four-year residential college. The reality, however, is a lot different. For one, many of those attending college today are not full-time students. In fact, about 37 percent of all undergraduates attend part-time. (At community colleges, nearly six of ten students attend on a part-time basis.) Most of those who attend part-time do so because they also work—and some of them work a lot. Nearly a third of all undergraduates work thirty-five hours a week or more. Many also have family responsibilities; nearly a quarter of them are parents, and more than one in eight is a single parent.[2]

The "typical" college student is also aging. More than a third of college students are aged twenty-five years and older, and that population of students has been growing at a faster rate than the number of younger students. This pattern is projected to continue, in part because colleges face a decline in high-school graduates over the next few years (the result of a broader demographic shift) and, as a result, will focus more on recruiting older students. Changes in the economy and high unemployment rates may also prompt adults to start or return to college for additional training and credentials.

Recently, however, that has not been the case. Between fall 2011 and fall 2013, college enrollment dropped, particularly among older students. Analysts speculate that with the economy improving, some of those adults were choosing work over school. For the decade ending in 2021, the National Center for Education Statistics has predicted a 13-percent increase in enrollments of students younger than twenty-five years and a rise of 14 percent in the enrollment of students aged twenty-five years and older. By 2021, it predicts that students older than twenty-five will compose about 42 percent of the college population.[3]

Age is not the only changing demographic. The American student body is also becoming more Hispanic. The number of Hispanic students in any level of higher education more than doubled from 1976 to about 782,000 in 1990 and then nearly quadrupled by 2012, reaching almost three million.[4] Young Hispanics are the fastest growing demographic in the country, and that is becoming increasingly apparent on college rosters. Thanks in part to improving high-school graduation rates, Hispanics now make up 19 percent of college students aged eighteen to twenty-four years, up from 12 percent in 2008. And they made up about 14 percent of all college students in 2012, up from 3.5 percent in 1976.[5]

But while Hispanics as a group have made the most notable gains in entering the higher education arena, they lag behind other groups when it comes to earning a bachelor's degree. In 2012, just 14.5 percent of Hispanics aged twenty-five years and older had a bachelor's degree, compared with 34.5 percent of whites and 21 percent of blacks. Among Asian Americans, 51 percent had a bachelor's degree.

The number of black students in higher education has increased, too, particularly since the mid-1990s, but not nearly at so fast a pace as that of Hispanics. Enrollment of black students nearly tripled between 1976 and 2012, to just short of three million. But as a percentage of the total student population, the increase was more modest. In 1976, of nearly eleven million students, black students accounted for just over 9 percent. Thirty-six years later, with about 20.6 million students in college, blacks made up only 14 percent of the overall student population.[6] While the reasons for the disparities in attainment are not entirely clear, experts note that some Hispanics may be following upward-mobility patterns that have been typical for other immigrant groups.

Experts expect this "browning" of higher education to continue for at least the next fifteen years, as the share of minority students in high school graduating classes grows. The Western Interstate Commission on Higher Education (WICHE), an organization of sixteen states and territories that tracks demographic trends of significance to education, predicts that by 2020, minority students (blacks, Hispanics, Asian Americans, and Pacific Islanders) will account for 45 percent of public high-school graduates, up from 38 percent in 2009. Most of those minorities earning high-school diplomas will be Hispanic students, although in some states, according to WICHE, even the term "minority" is already a misnomer. Nonwhite students now make up the majority of high-school graduates in

California, Hawaii, Mississippi, New Mexico, Texas, and the District of Columbia, and, according to WICHE's projections, by 2020, Arizona, Florida, Georgia, Maryland, and Nevada will join them.

For colleges, this shifting demographic tide poses particular challenges. As we will see later, many of these black and Hispanic students will be coming to college with less academic preparation and fewer resources to pay for it.

Enrollment has also shifted in terms of gender. Men once dominated higher education. That's no longer the case. After World War II, thanks in no small part to the educational benefits offered by the GI Bill, men outpaced women in earning bachelor's degrees by more than three to one. And they kept that lead over the next four decades, although the margin of difference grew smaller. But by 1982, women had overtaken men in overall bachelor's degrees conferred, and they continued to do so by increasingly wider margins. In 2009, of the more than 1.65 million bachelor's degrees awarded, nearly 57 percent went to women.[7] Today, in the college population, women continue to outnumber men by about four to three.[8]

Finally, about 4 percent of all undergraduates are military veterans, largely due to the Post-9/11 GI Bill, which has provided educational benefits to more than one million current and former members of the military services since summer 2009. Veterans' enrollment in higher education today is believed to be the highest, by proportion, since the years after World War II, when the original GI Bill brought more than two million veterans to college campuses.

How does the United States stack up internationally?

In the United States as of 2011, 42 percent of all adults aged twenty-five to sixty-four have a postsecondary education degree. That puts the United States fifth in terms of worldwide rates of college education, behind Canada (51 percent), Israel (46 percent), Japan (46 percent), and the Russian Federation

(53 percent), among the countries ranked by the Organization for Economic Cooperation and Development (OECD). But among younger adults, aged twenty-five to thirty-four, there are now eleven other countries with higher rates of college education, according to the OECD.[9]

The Paris-based OECD regularly assesses the education progress of its thirty-four member countries, as well as a few others. When the first of these "Education at a Glance" reports was published two decades ago, the United States ranked first in the proportion of all adults with a university-level education and first in the number of younger people with such an education. But comparisons between findings from the current OECD data with those in the first report, which covered 1991, are not clear-cut. For example, the 1991 report included data from just twenty countries. Also, until the late 1990s, OECD did not count associate degrees in the category of "university-level" education but rather put them in a category called "non-university tertiary education." In that category, several other countries surpassed the United States. And even with the two categories combined, Canada came out ahead. In other words, based on the standard by which most experts today look at postsecondary educational attainment—counting both associate and bachelor's degrees—the United States was actually never really number one in these OECD standings.

Still, America's "slide" in these worldwide rankings has become the cause for some public alarm, with politicians like U.S. Secretary of Education Arne Duncan suggesting that the country is growing "complacent" in its education standards.[10] But some analysts say the findings are not quite as dire as they appear. Several of the countries that now outrank the United States in the share of young people with college degrees also have fewer young people overall. According to Arthur M. Hauptman, an independent education-policy consultant, some of those countries are moving up in the rankings simply because their overall pool of young people has gotten smaller, not because they are educating that many more young people relative to their population.[11]

The New America Foundation's Kevin Carey, who directs the organization's Education Policy Program, says the comparisons the nation really has to worry about are those with the countries that rival the United States in economic power. America will still be in good shape, Carey wrote in *The Chronicle of Higher Education* in 2009, as long as the country can achieve better attainment rates for young people than countries like China, India, and the bulk of the European Union. (China and India are not in the OECD report; America's rate of 43 percent for those aged twenty-five to thirty-four is greater than that of the OECD and European Union averages but not that of Japan or Canada.)[12]

Why are there so many "goals" for raising the nation's college-going and college-attainment rates, and who sets them?

In February 2009, with the effects of the housing, unemployment, and financial crises of the Great Recession still unfolding, President Obama called on all Americans to commit to at least one year of postsecondary education. Standing before a joint session of Congress, the president stated: "This can be community college or a four-year school; vocational training or an apprenticeship. But whatever the training may be, every American will need to get more than a high school diploma." He also announced that the administration would develop policies that would ensure that "by 2020, America will once again have the highest proportion of college graduates in the world."

Some have presumed that this so-called 2020 Goal meant the White House was calling for "college for all," a notion that tends to draw more skepticism than enthusiasm. But in fact, that is not the case. As part of that goal, the White House has focused its attention on adults aged twenty-five to thirty-four and says it hopes to see the number of young people with a college degree increase by twenty-six million by 2020, eight million more than would be expected based on population growth and the past rate of attainment.

The educational aspirations for the nation set by the Obama administration were not unprecedented. In late 2008, a commission convened by the College Board and made up of some of the nation's most prominent college leaders announced a goal of at least 55 percent of Americans to hold a postsecondary credential by 2025, which they believed could be accomplished by increasing completion rates by 1 percent annually. A year before that commission's report, the Lumina Foundation for Education, a major philanthropy, had already begun talking about its own "Big Goal," which called for 60 percent of Americans to hold high-quality degrees, certificates, or other postsecondary credentials by 2025. That goal, which explicitly counts credentials that have value in the workplace and not just associate and bachelor's degrees, was later renamed Goal 2025.

Since then, more than a dozen states and educational groups have also adopted some versions of these goals. Few besides Lumina, however, have been especially vigilant about regularly reporting their progress toward meeting them. In its latest report, in mid-2013, Lumina found that the rate of college attainment in the United States is steadily improving but that the "pace of progress is far too modest to meet future workforce needs." It also found "massive and ongoing gaps in educational achievement—gaps tied to race, income, and other socioeconomic factors—that must be addressed."

As the Lumina report indicates, all of these types of goals are propelled largely by economic imperatives. Jobs of the future will require people with more education. Jobs that do not require as much education, such as those in low-skilled manufacturing, for example, are quickly disappearing. By some estimates, four of five of the jobs lost during the Great

Recession were those that required a high-school education or less. "Clearly, those low-skill jobs are gone for good," says Lumina.[13]

Of course, national pride also plays into the goals; as the College Board's commission put it in its report, "a compulsion to excel elsewhere in the world has transformed education globally; it is time we developed that same compulsion."[14]

Despite this and other such high-minded rhetoric around the goals, some policy experts have questioned their value. They note that a drive for more people with degrees without a commensurate focus on ensuring that the degrees are of high quality is not a true sign of educational progress. Other critics, like those at the John William Pope Center for Higher Education Quality, based in North Carolina, also argue that for some students, college could be just a costly waste of time. They contend that the economy cannot support that many college graduates. "Credential inflation has spread over the employment landscape just like kudzu over a field," the organization's research director, George Leef, wrote in a commentary in late 2013. "Owing to decades of pushing college as the path to success, we have so many graduates that employers can screen out anyone without a college degree—even for jobs that do not call for anything beyond basic trainability."[15] Indeed, the push for increasing the college-going rate has produced a bit of a backlash, prompting even the former secretary of education, William J. Bennett, to write a book in 2013 titled *Is College Worth It?* (His conclusion: It depends.)[16] Despite such concerns about the focus on degree rates, the 2020 goal remains a priority of the Obama administration.

How competitive is college admission?

For most of the nation's undergraduates, the admissions process is not as competitive as you might think. About 85 percent of 2,543 degree-granting four-year colleges accept at least half of all students who apply, and they account for about 80 percent of all four-year college undergraduate enrollments. Only about 2 percent of colleges accept less than a quarter of their applicants, and in fall 2011, those most-selective institutions accounted for the equivalent of just 4 percent of the undergraduate enrollment. In 2011, one of six students attended open-admissions four-year colleges—meaning their admissions criteria involved only the most basic of requirements.[17]

Yet there is no denying the admissions frenzy that surrounds the more-selective colleges. Fueled in part by the growing use of the Common Application, a service that began in 1975 with fifteen colleges and is now used by more than five hundred institutions, students today apply to many more colleges than they did in the past because they can easily submit most, if not all, of the same essays and application data to multiple colleges. The "Common App" first went online in 1998, after which, according to The Freshman Survey, the proportion of students applying to four-year colleges who applied to three or more institutions rose from 63 percent to 81 percent. The proportion of students applying to seven or more colleges rose from 11 percent to about 32 percent from 1998 to 2012.[18] Colleges are thus receiving far more applicants than in the past, meaning that acceptance rates are lower and competition for slots at elite schools has increased. For the class of 2018, Stanford University received more than 42,000 applications (a record) and admitted only 5 percent of them (also a record), while four Ivy League institutions—the University of Pennsylvania and Yale, Princeton, and Cornell Universities—all also reported their lowest admissions rates ever.[19] (As noted, however, such selectivity is atypical: Only about 17 percent of all public four-year colleges rejected even half of their applicants in 2011–2012, and among private four-year colleges, fewer than 20 percent did so.[20])

Warranted or not, the anxiety over admissions also feeds a growing college-counseling industry. This involves college guidebook publishers, countless college-search web sites (many of which make their money by offering greater visibility to colleges that advertise on them), and SAT and ACT tutoring services (which run the gamut from moonlighting high-school teachers to Wall Street–traded companies like those that own Kaplan Inc.'s test-preparation businesses and the Princeton Review) as well as the many independent consultants who charge families thousands of dollars to help students narrow their college choices, refine their essays, and ensure the applications are filed in time.

The size and reach of this diverse industry have only grown in recent years. In 2013, Kaplan's test-preparation businesses generated more than $293 million in revenues (although that sum includes its tutoring and large over-seas and graduate-school markets) while the Independent Educational Consultants Association (IECA) now counts more than one thousand advisors as members. Not all of the IECA members are college focused, but neither does this organiza-tion represent all the people out there who are selling coun-seling services to students and families. By one conservative, back-of-the-envelope estimate provided by a veteran of the college-prep industry, families are spending at least $500 mil-lion a year on such services. And that does not even reflect the spending by the hundreds of nonprofit organizations associ-ated with the National College Access Network (including one modeled after Teach for America called the National College Advising Corps), which concentrate their activities on advis-ing lower-income students.

Why do some analysts call higher education an "engine of inequality"?

As a group, wealthier people have always been better educated than low-income people. College opportunity in the United States has expanded, but it has done little to substantially alter that dynamic. Over the past two generations, as the baby boom-ers and their children flooded colleges, people from the sector of society with the lowest income have made gains in college attainment, but not nearly at the same rate as have those from the high-income sector. Between 1970 and 2012, the proportion of students graduating from high school from the quarter of the population with the lowest income increased from about 62 percent to 72 percent. Yet over those same forty-two years, the proportion of low-income twenty-four-year-olds (family income of $34,160 and below) with bachelor's degrees went from just 6 percent to slightly over 8 percent. Meanwhile, the proportion of upper income twenty-four-year-olds (family income of $108,650 and up) with a bachelor's degree increased from 40 percent to 73 percent.[21]

Those data come from the Pell Institute for the Study of Opportunity in Higher Education, an independent nonprofit organization. The organization is named after Claiborne Pell, the now-deceased six-term U.S. senator from Rhode Island who championed the creation of a federal program that provides aid for needy college students. Pell Grants began reaching all eligible students in the mid-1970s, and in the subsequent forty-plus years, the program has grown exponentially. It now serves more than nine million students a year at an annual cost of about $35 billion. Between 2008 and 2012 alone, federal spending on Pell Grants doubled.

As the institute's data and other studies show, however, even the expansion of the Pell Grant program has not compensated for inequities in family wealth. U.S. Department of Education data on students who enrolled in college immediately after high school, for example, shows that in 2011, 82 percent of high-income students went on to college while only 52 percent of low-income students did. In 1975, overall figures were lower, but the difference was virtually the same.[22]

It is not just a question of access to college. One study by Martha J. Bailey and Susan M. Dynarski, professors at the University of Michigan, found "increasing advantage" over time for students from upper-income families when it came to students not just entering but also completing college.[23]

Likewise, a Pell Institute analysis found that when it came to bachelor's degrees, the share of twenty-four-year-olds with such a degree rose from 44 percent to 54 percent from 1980 to 2011 for those in the top income quartile, while for families in the bottom half, it actually fell by 5 percentage points to 22 percent. Mortenson, the senior scholar at the institute, says that even for students who make it into college, those from highest economic quartile are now about four times as likely to complete their bachelor's degree by age twenty-four than those from the bottom quartile, a ratio that has grown since about 1980.[24]

Why is this the case? Even with the expansion of the Pell Grant program, state financial aid programs, outside scholarships, and the grants offered by colleges, the financial and academic-preparedness barriers loom large for many students from low-income families. But that is just one aspect of the problem. Students from disadvantaged families often do not get timely advice on what high-school classes they must take to qualify for admission to a four-year college, what standardized tests they need to sign up for, or how to fill out the form that is the gateway to federal student aid, the *Free Application for Federal Student Aid* (FAFSA).

Experts call this body of information "college knowledge," and many have now come to believe that students need exposure to it as early as middle school. The reason is not only to introduce high aspirations but also because in some cases, students who do not take the right preparatory classes then will be denied access to Advanced Placement courses later. There exists a whole coterie of organizations interested in the issue, such as the Institute for Higher Education Policy and the Council for Opportunity in Education, and a number of federally financed programs—like Gear Up and Upward Bound, as well as community-based ones like College Bound in Washington, D.C.—that work hands-on with students on writing, mathematics, and other skills to address these gaps. The many nonprofit "access" organizations are making a dent in addressing education inequality, but experts estimate that fewer than one in seven high-need students are served by one of these groups.

Arnold L. Mitchem, founder of the Council for Opportunity in Education and the man credited with coining the term "first-generation college student," says that when it comes to helping low-income students get into and succeed in college, "the record remains fairly dismal." The nation has improved financial aid, he says, but has yet to systematically align it with the support services that some of the financially neediest students need to navigate college admission and completion.

What is the effect of merit scholarship programs?

Financial aid comes in two basic forms. One is need-based aid, which is awarded by both colleges and governments based on students' financial situations. The other, known as "merit aid," or scholarships, is awarded by colleges to athletes, high-achieving students, musicians, and students with other traits that colleges find desirable. Many states also have merit-aid programs that award grants to students based on criteria other than pure financial need. Private organizations also offer scholarships, based on a range of criteria.

The rise of merit aid is a well-documented and much-debated phenomenon. Between 1996 and 2008, the share of students receiving merit aid from private colleges out of their own coffers grew from 24 percent to 44 percent, while at public colleges the share rose from 8 to 18 percent, according to a report by the National Center for Educational Statistics.[25] The rise has been seen at the state level as well, where merit aid programs, like Georgia's Hope Scholarships, are popular with politicians looking to connect with their middle-class constituents. That interest is reflected in how states distribute their aid dollars: Prior to 1992, merit scholarships accounted for less than 10 percent of state spending on undergraduate aid, but they now account for about a quarter of those expenditures. Advocates for needy students have decried the shift in spending away from need-based aid and may well have been heartened when in 2011–2012, states reported a slight reversal in the share of the $9.4 billion of state aid for undergraduates going for merit scholarships.

Yet, as the New America Foundation's Stephen Burd found in a 2013 report that received widespread attention, when it comes to deciding how to allocate their own money, some colleges provide merit aid to their wealthier students while charging their neediest students tuition that takes a painful bite out of their family's income. Such colleges, says Burd, use their merit aid as "a competitive weapon" to attract students who can pay more while endangering a pathway to the middle class for low-income and working-class students.[26] Burd's study looked at 479 private colleges and found 61 percent of them were charging $15,000 or more to students from families with incomes of $30,000 or less. In other words, they were asking families to provide more than half of their family income to pay for the child's college costs. The $15,000-plus was the average "net price" those students were being asked to pay, after taking into account all other federal, state, and institutional aid the students were awarded. Twenty-two percent of those 479 colleges were charging needy students $20,000 a year (two-thirds of their entire family income), while at the same time providing merit aid to more than one of five of their students. This is particularly worrisome because studies show that students faced with high net costs end up graduating at lower rates.[27]

Burd also looked at 480 public four-year colleges. The results there were less severe—34 percent charged their neediest students a net price over $10,000 and only 5 percent charged $15,000 or more.[28] (Quirks in the way some colleges award financial aid have prompted some colleges to take issue with Burd's findings about particular institutions, although not with his overall conclusions.) Burd's report points to the fact that colleges leverage their financial aid budgets to benefit students who do not actually need the aid—often in hopes of bringing in top students to raise the college's rankings or to appeal to wealthier students whose families can afford to pay the rest of the price not covered by the merit aid.

The report also singled out an increasingly influential player in the admissions-and-financial-aid process as a culprit: the enrollment-management industry. "Enrollment management" is a broad term for the array of marketing and finance consultants and companies that strategize behind the scenes at many colleges to help them get the size and profile of the class they want and make their revenue goals. They advise on where to recruit students and develop techniques to help identify applicants most likely to enroll. Often, their strategies extend to proposals for new merit-aid programs— automatic "presidential scholarships" for high-school students with B averages and above, for example—designed to attract an applicant who will be flattered enough by the offer to consider the college.

Properly deployed, these enrollment management techniques can help tuition-dependent colleges from discounting so much that they become financially unstable—a danger that is growing for many private colleges (as we will see in the section that follows on costs). But they can also have a pernicious effect at institutions with only so much money to give away in scholarships. That is because, as Burd says, despite the label, "the money doesn't always go to the meritorious."[29] Of the full-time students receiving merit aid studied in a 2011 National Center for Educational Statistics report, 19 percent had combined SAT scores below 700 (of a possible 1,600) and 20 percent had a grade point average below a C.[30]

Even college leaders who claim to dislike the practice of giving merit-based aid say they now continue it as a necessary evil. As a college president told colleagues a couple of years ago at a meeting: "Wealthy families want to sit at the country club and say, 'My kid got a merit scholarship.'"[31]

Is American higher education racially and economically segregated?

"Separate and unequal" was the indictment of public schools during the era of legal segregation. Today, some scholars use the same language to describe the stratification taking place in postsecondary education. The economic disparities are incontrovertible: as more and more lower-income people have enrolled in higher education, four-year colleges have become increasingly the preserve of more-affluent students while community colleges and for-profit colleges, which spend less per student on instruction, enroll the preponderance of the financially neediest students.

Those who study economic-equity issues in elementary and secondary education often use data on the number of children eligible for free or reduced lunches as a guide for measuring financial need. In higher education, the proxy is often which students are eligible for Pell Grants. Today, more than half of all students, or 52 percent, are Pell Grant eligible. (In primary and secondary schools nationwide, 53 percent of students participating in the federal school lunch program qualified for free or reduced-price meals in 2012, a harbinger of the poverty-related issues that colleges, and governments, will face in the years to come.)[32]

When the Pell Grant program began in the 1970s, just over a quarter of the eight million or so undergraduates received the grants. At the time, six of ten Pell Grant recipients were enrolled in four-year colleges. That share began to slide in 1980, and according to the Pell Institute, by 2011 fewer than four of ten Pell recipients attended a four-year college.[33] That slide also corresponds with an expansive shift in higher education. Between 1980 and 2011, the undergraduate higher education population nearly doubled, growing from 9.4 million to 18.1 million. Students from needy families accounted for nearly all of that growth—and the number of undergraduates with Pell Grants rose from 2.7 million to 9.4 million during that period.[34]

Where did all of these Pell Grant–eligible students go to school? Mostly they went to community and for-profit colleges. The number of Pell Grant recipients at community colleges increased by 2.7 million between 1980 and 2011, a figure that is about equal to the overall increase in enrollment at those two-year colleges. The share of Pell Grant recipients attending for-profit colleges went from about 11 percent in 1980 to more than 23 percent by 2011.[35] The result is a higher education landscape deeply stratified along economic lines.

The view through a racial/ethnic lens paints an equally dismal picture, so much so that scholars at the Georgetown University Center on Education and the Workforce say the postsecondary system now "mimics the racial inequality it inherits from the K-12 education system, then magnifies and projects that inequality into the labor market and society at large."[36]

This is not an issue of basic access to a college education. As those Georgetown scholars say in their 2013 "Separate and Unequal" report, between 1995 and 2009, new freshmen enrollments grew by 197 percent for Hispanic students and 73 percent for African American students, far outpacing the 15-percent increase in white students. But *where* those students went to college differed greatly by ethnicity. Most of the white students went to one of the nation's 468 more-selective public and private four-year colleges, while most of the Hispanic and African American students ended up at open-access two-year and four-year institutions.[37]

As a result, at those 468 more-selective colleges, where about 20 percent of all freshmen are enrolled, whites were overrepresented relative to their share of the college-age population, while African Americans and Hispanics were underrepresented. (As the report showed, whites make up 62 percent of the college-age population but 75 percent of the students at the more-selective institutions. African American and Hispanic students make up 33 percent of the college-age population but only 14 percent of the students at these more-selective colleges.) At community colleges and open-access institutions, whites are disproportionately underrepresented, while African American and Hispanic students are overrepresented.

The divergent paths have a quantifiable impact on students' opportunity for upward mobility, say the report's authors, Anthony P. Carnevale, director of the center at Georgetown, and Jeffrey Strohl. The more-selective institutions spend three to five times as much per student on instruction than the open-access colleges, have higher graduation rates, and send more students on to graduate school. Ten years after finishing college, the graduates of those more-selective institutions also out-earn those from an open-access college, by an average of $67,000 to $49,000.

Carnevale and Strohl found that for high-achieving African American and Hispanic students who managed to attend one of the more-selective institutions rather than an open-access college, there were "enormous benefits." For one, they were nearly twice as likely to graduate. They were also more likely to go on to graduate school. Those who miss out on these benefits, in contrast, are likely to face real economic losses. The center calculates that workers with advanced degrees earn up to $2.1 million more than college dropouts over a lifetime.

This "racially polarized" system carries potential ramifications for the next generation as well, because children's education levels are often driven by those of their parents. Statistics in the "Separate and Unequal" report show that white students with college-educated parents are eight times as likely to have earned a bachelor's degree or higher as are African American or Hispanic students whose parents have a high-school degree or less, and three times as likely than African American or Hispanic students whose parents dropped out of college or earned only an associate degree. The Carnevale and Strohl study shows that students who do not attend a more-selective institution are less likely to graduate and, therefore, also are at a higher risk of raising children who themselves will not get a degree. And a disproportionate number of those students are African American and Hispanic.

Where do community colleges fit in this picture?

Community colleges have expanded steadily since the 1960s and in a few cases now even provide four-year degrees along with their traditional offerings of associate degrees in academic and technical fields as well as certificates in subjects like construction and other trades. With 40 percent of all undergraduates attending community colleges, these schools do much of higher education's heavy lifting. Even their strongest supporters acknowledge that too many of them are struggling under that weight. Eight of ten students enter community colleges expecting to transfer and earn a bachelor's degree, but only about 17 percent ultimately do so within six years, according to the National Student Clearinghouse Research Center.[38]

The students at community colleges are the neediest financially and the least academically prepared, yet these colleges spend less per student on educational costs, on average, than public or private institutions. That disparity, along with research showing that community college enrollments in some cases were overwhelmingly made up of minority students, is what prompted a Century Foundation task force in 2013 to decry what it called "the increasing economic and racial isolation of students" at community colleges. In a report that warned that community colleges "are in great danger of becoming indelibly separate and unequal institutions in the higher-education landscape," the task force argued for new efforts at community colleges, such as the establishment of honors programs, to encourage more academically prepared middle-class and nonminority students to enroll. It also called on four-year colleges, particularly elite ones, to seek out more community college students as transfers.[39] Finally, it called for a higher-education version of "adequacy-based" funding programs (similar to the federal program known as Title I at the elementary and secondary-school level) that the U.S. government and some states now use to provide extra money to public schools that enroll high numbers of students in poverty. The proposal, while a dramatic statement of the task force's sense of the seriousness of the problem, is unlikely to gain traction in Washington's current budget-cutting climate.

Are for-profit colleges also affected by this race and class divide?

In a word, yes. However, it is important to recognize that the for-profit-college sector, which runs the gamut from mega-universities owned by Wall Street titans to family-owned ventures, is no more monolithic than higher education as a whole. Some for-profit colleges offer bachelor's and master's degrees (like DeVry University) and a few even offer doctorates (University of Phoenix and Capella University), and those institutions attract a different study body, demographically, than the schools often described as "career colleges" that offer certificates in medical coding or training for technicians in heating, ventilation, and air-conditioning. Yet as a group, for-profit colleges attract a disproportionate share of minority and low-income students.

An enrollment shift to for-profit colleges from public colleges began in 2000. At first, it was most pronounced among low-income white students. In 2000, 22 percent of low-income white students attended four-year public colleges and 10 percent enrolled in for-profits. (Most of the rest were enrolled in community colleges.) By 2008, the share of low-income whites at public colleges had fallen to 14 percent and had risen to 16 percent at for-profit colleges. Poor students from other racial and ethnic groups were already making up a significant share of for-profit enrollments in 2000. But over the succeeding eight years, their presence grew even larger, too. In 2000, about one third of low-income students who were black or Hispanic enrolled in for-profit colleges. In 2008, nearly half of them did.[40]

The Institute for Higher Education Policy, the organization that analyzed this enrollment shift, also found a "pronounced overrepresentation" of low-income women at for-profit colleges. In 2008 low-income women were three times as likely as their higher-income counterparts to enroll at a for-profit college, the institute found. Despite the fact that for-profit colleges make up the smallest sector of higher education, the institute also found that more low-income black and Hispanic women were enrolled in for-profit colleges than in four-year public and private colleges combined.

By themselves, those trends could be viewed a testament to the efforts that the for-profit-college industry has made toward attracting so-called underrepresented student populations. But the value of a for-profit college education is very much in question. These colleges typically cost much more than community colleges or public four-year institutions (on average more than four times the cost of a community college for an associate degree),[41] and the students who attend them borrow far more money for tuition and default on their loans at higher rates than most other students. And according to some analysts, graduates of for-profit schools fare less well in the job market than those from nonprofit colleges with comparable training. A 2012 study that looked at for-profit students and similar kinds of students at community colleges and public and private four-year colleges, for example, found that while the rates of student retention were higher at for-profit colleges, the students who attended them had lower rates of employment and lower salaries six years after they entered college.[42]

For-profit degrees may also carry an extra stigma. A 2014 survey by Public Agenda of employers and for-profit-college alumni found that employers were more likely to favor applicants from nonprofit institutions over those from for-profits. (It also found that current for-profit-college students were generally satisfied with their education but just 37 percent of for-profit alumni said their degree was worth the price, and four in ten said their colleges were more concerned about making money than about educating students.)[43]

As critics view it, the concentration of low-income and minority students at for-profit colleges is a sign that the industry has been successful in aiming its aggressive, and in some cases predatory, recruiting tactics at students with the least information about how best to select a college and the fewest resources to pay for it. This is worrisome, as these findings on enrollment shifts suggest that the growing dependence on for-profit colleges by students from low-income families may adversely affect their chances of completing college, managing their student-loan debts, and finding a good job.

Haven't affirmative action efforts over the past few decades helped make colleges more diverse?

In many cases, campuses may look and be more diverse now than a few generations ago, but that diversity goes only so far. As noted previously, campuses are now more stratified by income levels than ever before, and this lack of socioeconomic diversity is especially acute at the most-selective institutions. Racial diversity is also lacking on selective campuses—as mentioned, African American and Hispanic students make up 33 percent of the college-age population but only 14 percent of the students at more-selective colleges—but experts say minorities would be underrepresented in even greater

numbers than they are now had colleges not begun using
affirmative action in admissions.

While it is still controversial in some quarters, colleges
have been using affirmative action in admissions for nearly
fifty years. The U.S. Supreme Court first weighed in on its use
in higher education in the 1987 *Bakke* decision arising from
a case at the University of California. That decision banned
the use of admissions quotas as tools for affirmative action
but confirmed colleges' right to consider an applicant's race
in an effort to achieve a more diverse student body. In the
decades that followed, however, several high-profile legal
challenges and political battles chipped away at affirmative
action. In 1996, California voters adopted Proposition 209,
which prohibited public bodies from considering race, sex, or
ethnicity in hiring or admissions. That same year, state officials in Texas determined that a federal appeals court ruling
known as *Hopwood v. Texas* meant that no university in the
state could use such considerations in admissions either. The
Hopwood ruling applied in Louisiana and Mississippi as well.
In 1998, voters in Washington State approved their own ban
on affirmative action, and lawmakers in Florida approved one
the following year. Another federal appeals court decision,
growing out of the University of Georgia in 2001 and known
as the *Johnson* ruling, imposed limits on affirmative action in
Georgia, Alabama, and Florida.

In those eight states where the bans and rulings were in
effect, most universities diminished their use of affirmative action. They did so even though a pair of U.S. Supreme
Court rulings in 2003, arising from the University of Michigan
(*Grutter v. Bollinger* and *Gratz v. Bollinger*), narrowly upheld the
use of race-conscious policies in admissions, as long as they
were part of a holistic consideration of individual applicants.

The effect of affirmative action is hard to assess because
colleges are not always straightforward about whether, and
to what extent, they are using it. But experts say one way to
measure its effect on diversity is to examine places where

affirmative action is known to have once been used, and then halted. A study published in 2014 by two researchers at the University of Washington did just that—and found that in states where affirmative action remained in force over time, minority admissions were notably higher than in states where the practice has been banned.[44]

The University of Washington researchers compared admissions patterns for equally qualified minority and non-minority students in the eight states where court rulings or legal bans limited affirmative action with those in the forty other states in the continental United States. Comparing data from 1992 and then 2004, by which time the bans had all been in effect, the researchers found substantial declines in levels of minority-student admissions to selective colleges in the eight states affected by the bans and judicial rulings, "and no evidence of declines outside these states." Affirmative action policies made a difference where they were in effect, says Marc C. Long, one of the researchers. Diversity on those campuses "would be much worse without it."[45]

Since 2003, voters in four other states have approved state-wide bans on affirmative action: Michigan and Nebraska in 2006, Arizona in 2010, and Oklahoma in 2012. An affirmative action ban proposed in Colorado was defeated by voters in 2008. A case challenging the Michigan ban was heard by the Supreme Court in October 2013, and in April 2014, the court upheld the ban in a six-to-two ruling. In 2014, California lawmakers considered a measure to be placed on the November ballot to revoke Proposition 209 with respect to education, but the sponsor later withdrew it after finding that it was unlikely to pass.

Will the U.S. Supreme Court's ruling in the Fisher v. University of Texas at Austin case make it less likely that colleges will actively recruit minority students?

The *Fisher* case, which was argued before the Supreme Court in October 2012, was brought by Abigail Noel Fisher, a white applicant who was denied admission to the University of Texas at Austin in 2008 as an undergraduate. Fisher did not qualify for automatic admission under the university's "top 10 percent" plan, so she was considered as part of another pool, where students were evaluated based on criteria that gave extra consideration to black and Hispanic applicants. (The university had been one of the few in Texas to reinstitute affirmative action in its admissions process after the Supreme Court's 2003 decisions.) Fisher challenged the university's admissions practices as a violation of the U.S. Constitution's equal protection clause.

The U.S. district and appeals courts that heard her case sided with the university, which had argued that its consideration of race in admissions was necessary. When the conservative-leaning Supreme Court took the case, many court watchers predicted that it was doing so to clamp down on affirmative action. Instead, in a seven-to-one ruling, the court appeared to sidestep the issue. It determined that the lower courts had deferred too readily to the university's judgment. "The reviewing court must ultimately be satisfied that no workable race-neutral alternatives would produce the educational benefits of diversity," Justice William Kennedy wrote for the majority, and the case was sent back to the U.S. Court of Appeals for the Fifth Circuit.[46]

Still, commentators and analysts say the language of the ruling, which noted that race-conscious policies are subject to strict court scrutiny, could ultimately open the door to many more challenges to admissions policies that take race into consideration. Indeed, several groups, including the one that helped Fisher bring her case, have said they plan such challenges. It is therefore quite possible that ruling will affect schools' recruiting of minority students; at the very least, it will require universities to be more diligent in documenting their rationale for using affirmative action in admissions to increase racial diversity.

What is "undermatching," and what role does it play in higher-education diversity?

In many middle- and upper-class communities, the students with the best grades typically aspire to and attend the most selective colleges. A growing body of research now shows the same is not true for top minority students and top students who come from low-income households. They are said to be victims of "undermatching," because they do not end up at the more-selective colleges that they are qualified to attend.

This occurs in part because many of the top minority students who would qualify for admission to selective colleges simply do not apply to them, choosing instead to attend colleges with less-rigorous requirements because they are closer to their home, or they think they will be less expensive. (While Burd's aforementioned study showed that some top colleges are not all that generous, some of the most selective colleges do offer needy students more-than-adequate financial aid packages.) For all the talk about American higher education being a meritocracy, data showing the prevalence of this "undermatching" is another sign of the inequities in the system.

The problem of undermatching first gained national attention in a 2009 book, *Crossing the Finish Line: Completing College at America's Public Universities*, which looked at students at twenty-one flagship universities and forty-seven other public universities in four states and found strong disparities in graduation rates based on students' race, ethnicity, and socioeconomic status.[47] It then became an even more prominent issue in 2013, after researchers Caroline M. Hoxby and Christopher Avery made a splash with a more expansive study on what they called "the hidden supply" of high-achieving students from low-income households.[48]

Hoxby and Avery combed through data on students from the lowest quartile by household income (at or below $41,472) who ranked in the top 10 percent based on their grade-point average and their SAT or ACT scores.[49] They estimated there were between 25,000 and 35,000 high-achieving, low-income high-school seniors in 2008 but that the majority of them did not apply to top colleges. Had they attended there, the study says, the students would have also been likely to succeed academically. By contrast, the top-achieving students from upper-income families followed typical advice of admission counselors and applied to a range of colleges where they would be likely to be admitted, based on their grades and test scores, as well as some "safety schools" and "reach schools."

In her study of nine hundred valedictorians from public high schools, Alexandria Walton Radford, the author of *Top Student, Top School?* reported a similar trend. Only half of the valedictorians from working-class or low-income families applied to the sixty-one most-selective colleges on the *U.S. News & World Report* rankings, but of those from upper-middle class and upper-income families, four of five did so.[50]

While some admissions officers at selective colleges say they end up enrolling small numbers of low-income students because there are few such students who would qualify for admission, Hoxby and Avery say the colleges could do more to find them. "Many colleges look for low-income students where the college is instead of looking for low-income students where the students are," they note.[51] Many of these students may fail to apply to such colleges because they are never advised to do so. They often come from cash-strapped high schools where guidance counselors typically serve more than three hundred students at a time and from households where family members do not know about selective colleges. Hoxby and Avery say these students are "invisible to admissions staff" at colleges and are unlikely to come to their attention through traditional recruiting channels.

In collaboration with the College Board, Hoxby and others are now testing a number of low-cost strategies—like mailing customized information to students on what their likely costs of college would be and offering application-fee waivers—to close this information gap and encourage more top students to apply to more-selective colleges. President Obama gave additional visibility to the issue of undermatching in January 2014, when he and Michelle Obama invited more than one hundred college presidents and leaders of forty other organizations to a White House Summit on "Expanding College Opportunity." The attendees and others were asked to offer public pledges describing the ways they would increase enrollment of disadvantaged students.

While many higher-education experts have praised this attention to the undermatching issue, some leaders of non-elite colleges that already attract many low-income students, including a coalition called Yes We Must, say their efforts at serving low-income and minority students have been overlooked by policy makers. Additionally, some experts argued that the attention is misdirected. Worrying about the undermatch at Princeton, for example, or even at less-selective state universities, "is a distraction from the real work ahead—accurately measuring and then improving the success of graduates from broad-access institutions such as UT Brownsville or DeVry," according to Schneider, the former commissioner of education statistics and a vice president at the American Institutes for Research. Such broad-access institutions, he notes, can "open doors for many more low-income students than the more selective institutions will ever educate, and improving graduation rates at regional campuses or for-profit institutions is essential to increasing the number of adults with postsecondary credentials."[52]

How many students come to college prepared to do college-level work? What happens to those who are not prepared?

On the surface, it appears that many students come to college unprepared to succeed. More than half of the students at two-year colleges and nearly 20 percent of those at four-year colleges are placed in remedial classes. But according to various studies, some of the students assigned to such classes, typically based on standardized placement tests, do not belong in them and would do just as well without them.

Preparation levels are notably lower among first-generation college students. In 2013, the nonprofit organization ACT, which also administers the ACT college entrance tests, found only 9 percent of first-generation would-be college students met the college-readiness benchmarks in all four subjects that it evaluates (English, reading, mathematics, and science) compared with 26 percent of all students taking the test. More than half of the first-generation students did not meet even one benchmark.

ACT research has found that students who take a rigorous core curriculum in high school tend to be better prepared for college.[53] But providing such curricula is not always easily accomplished at some of the poorly funded high schools where first-generation students, who often come from low-income and minority families, attend. This is affirmed by the disparities in race and income levels of students who are assigned to remedial courses in college. A study by Complete College America found that at two-year colleges, nearly 68 percent of African American students, 58 percent of Hispanic students, and 65 percent of Pell Grant–eligible students were assigned to remedial classes, while at four-year colleges, the rates were 39, 20, and 31 percent, respectively.[54]

Unfortunately, studies suggest that remedial classes may not be an effective solution for struggling students. In its "Bridge to Nowhere" report, Complete College America says many college remedial courses are poorly conceived and become "dead ends" for students. Many of the students assigned to those classes never actually enroll in them at all, choosing instead to leave school or muddle through without them. And even when students do enroll, the classes do not always help: Fewer than 10 percent of students who take a remedial class at community college graduate within three years, and at four-year colleges, only a little more than one-third graduate within six years.[55]

Findings like these have led Complete College America to call for dramatic changes to improve remedial education, such as eliminating the courses altogether and replacing them with "just-in-time" tutoring (provided ad hoc when students need help with specific topics in other courses) and other services to help students succeed in credit-bearing courses. While a number of other organizations have taken issue with this tough-love approach, few say the current system, which by some estimates costs states and students $3 billion a year, is a satisfactory one.

Are distance-education courses or "alternative-education" approaches effective for students from educationally disadvantaged backgrounds?

Courses and degrees offered online or in other distance-education formats that do not require face-to-face interaction with instructors and so-called alternative-education approaches such as competency-based education, where students earn credits by proving that they have mastered skills regardless of how much time it takes them, are beginning to take hold in American higher education. However, what little research there is on the efficacy of such alternative education for disadvantaged students has not been promising. Analyses by the Community College Research Center have found that community college students, who are more likely to be low-income and less-prepared academically, withdraw from online courses at a higher rate compared with face-to-face classes. The center, which reviewed dozens of small-scale studies to draw its conclusions, also found that students in online classes—as well as those in other kinds of courses with less structure, less academic support, and fewer social connections—may become more discouraged and fail to return and progress in their education. A study based on students at twenty-three Virginia community colleges found, for example, that students who had taken remedial English classes online later had lower success rates in the college-level course than those who took the classes face to face; those with more online courses were also less likely to transfer to a four-year college.[56]

Additionally, for some students, just getting connected to the online class could be a problem. Today, seven of ten adults aged eighteen or older have broadband access, but as with educational attainment and college-going patterns, there are disparities that cut along racial and economic lines—a situation sometimes referred to as the "bandwidth divide." According to a May 2013 survey by the Pew Internet & American Life Project, little more than half of all adults with incomes under $30,000 have high-speed Internet connection in their homes, compared with 88 percent of those with incomes above $75,000. Among whites surveyed, 74 percent had broadband; among Hispanics, about half had it; and among blacks, the figure was 64 percent.[57] Such realities limit the ability of alternative-education approaches like online courses to reach low-income students, who in theory could benefit most from the potential flexibility in scheduling and lower costs of such offerings.

Part Two

COSTS, SPENDING, AND DEBT

How much does America spend on higher education, and how has that changed over time?

Higher education is big business. The nearly $500 billion in revenues generated annually by colleges and universities represented about 3 percent of the nation's gross domestic product in 2012, roughly the same size as the country's entertainment, arts, and culture industries combined. In raw dollars that is nearly double what it was through most of the 1990s. And it has only been increasing; from 1969 through 2012, higher-education spending increased by an annual average of 7 percent a year. The rise in enrollments that has driven this growth is already beginning to reverse slightly, and a tapering is expected to continue for the next decade. Still, analysts project that from now to 2022, the revenues spent on higher education will increase by about 3 percent annually, growing to $650 billion a year.[1]

Some of the recent growth in education spending was driven by for-profit colleges, where enrollments increased at a much faster pace during this period than in higher-education as a whole. By one conservative count, enrollment at for-profit colleges rose from approximately a half-million students in the mid-1990s to 2.4 million in fall 2011, counting students both at degree-granting institutions and at institutions that offer certificates and other postsecondary credentials. The for-profit-college sector now accounts for between 5 and 6 percent of all higher-education revenues, up from about 1 percent in the late 1990s. Yet since 2011, college enrollment has dropped most steeply at for-profit colleges as concern about students' high debt loads and government scrutiny of the sector—and media coverage of those issues—has intensified.

Besides tuition, what are other sources of income for colleges?

Except for a lucky few dozen of the wealthiest colleges, tuition is the major source of revenue for all colleges. This dependency on tuition is becoming increasingly significant even for public colleges, which used to get a bigger share of their operating support from state funds.

When it comes to discussions on college finances, though, that is about where the commonality ends. That is because the revenue streams that make up the budget for a private research university, which typically gets the rest of its income via gifts from its wealthy alumni, federal grants, and hospital fees if it has one, are far different than those of, say, a regional public college. The make-up of revenues is so different, in fact, that the most authoritative source on college costs and spending, the Delta Cost Project, breaks its analyses into seven categories for the different kinds of colleges. For example, tuition accounted for less than one-fifth of revenues at private research universities in 2011, while at public universities that offer only bachelor's and master's degrees, it accounted for about a third of all revenues.[2] Likewise, at public research universities, government grants and appropriations made up more than one-fifth of the revenues while at private bachelor's institutions they account for only about 3 percent.[3]

Another source of revenue is endowments, although not to the extent that most people believe. While endowments do play a crucial rule in funding for some institutions, those represent a small minority of the higher-education universe. Ten institutions have endowments big enough, in theory, to cover more than 45 percent of their operating budgets, according to data compiled by Moody's Investors Service: Princeton Theological Seminary; Grinnell College; Franklin Olin College of Engineering; Pomona College; Princeton University; Berea, Swarthmore, Williams, and Amherst Colleges; and the Juilliard School. (Harvard, the wealthiest of all, comes in eleventh, along with Rice University—each with endowments large enough to cover 39 percent.) Overall, fewer than three dozen of some 1,600 private colleges have endowments big enough to spin off enough income to cover at least a quarter of their annual operating budgets.[4] But in reality few if any actually use even that much. On average colleges rely on endowment income to cover 9 percent of their budgets, according to the National Association of College and University Business Officers.

Additionally, endowments are not big slush funds. Typically they comprise numerous smaller funds that can only be spent for specific purposes often set by donors. By some estimates, nearly 80 percent of public-college endowment assets carry some restriction on how their earnings can be used—some funds, for example, are designated for student aid, others for research, others for the library. At private colleges, restrictions cover about 55 percent of endowment assets.[5]

Still, there *are* colleges in the U.S. with very large endowments—in June 2007, seventy-four colleges had endowments worth $1 billion or more, and Harvard and Yale had endowments worth more than $35 billion and $22 billion, respectively.[6] Before the financial crisis, the great wealth that these colleges had amassed (tax free) in their endowments did not go unnoticed. Critics, most visibly U.S. Senator Charles Grassley (R-Iowa), publicly questioned whether colleges with such wealth should be required to spend at least 5 percent of their endowment value each year, just as foundations are required to do under federal tax laws. He focused primarily on the 136 institutions with endowments worth $500 million and up. But higher-education leaders argued that such a rule would not necessarily result in lower costs for students because most endowment income is designated for particular purposes and is not fungible. They also said that in years when endowment values fell, such a rule could force colleges to undermine the value of funds meant to serve future generations of students.

Endowment values have also soared and sunk with the rest of the market in the past few years. Average endowment investments returns have ranged from a high of 17 percent in 2007 to negative 19 percent in 2009. For the year ending June 2013, the average investment return for endowments was 11.7 percent. With these ups and downs, the public pressure on colleges to spend more from their endowments has mostly eased even though, according to the latest data, in 2013 there were eighty universities in the United States with endowments worth $1 billion or more and 151 with endowments worth more than $500 million, more in each case than when Senator Grassley first took on the issue.[7]

In addition to the direct benefits that accrue to colleges with large endowments, those institutions also enjoy some indirect advantages. A 2007 report from the Congressional Research Service found that earnings from these colleges' accumulated endowment value of $340 billion cost the government $18 billion in revenue, based on an investment return of 15 percent. (That was right before the financial crisis when returns were consistently strong for several years.) This is because earnings from those endowments are largely exempt from federal income tax. Since most institutions do not have large endowments, however, that is a tax benefit that carries little impact for them.[8]

What impact do donations have on college revenues?

Ultimately, when it comes to higher-education philanthropy, it is mostly a story of the rich getting richer. In 2013 colleges collectively received more than $33.8 billion in donations—a record. But generally the big money goes to the biggest and most established institutions, typically a handful of elite liberal arts colleges and universities with major research programs and hospitals. Indeed in 2013, ten institutions, all of them private research universities, accounted for about 17 percent of the reported total donated to higher education, according to the Council on Aid to Education.

Also, as the council has reported, the average gift to private research universities ($128,000 in 2012) was typically about twice the size of that at public research universities, eleven times the size of the average gift to private four-year colleges, more than thirty times the size of the average gift to four-year public colleges, and more than one hundred times the size of the average gift to community colleges.[9] The largest gifts are therefore concentrated at the very top; although between 2000 and 2012 donors gave over 10,500 gifts each worth at least $1 million (totaling more than $90 billion), less than a third of all colleges were on the receiving end of that largesse. The beneficiaries that fared best in this rarified pool were those that tended to be older (those founded before 1900 received more and bigger gifts), were growing in enrollment, had more full-time faculty, and had bigger endowments.[10]

The fundraising consulting firm Marts & Lundy, which saw 2013 as the year mega-gifts "came roaring back" following several down years during the financial crisis, predicts this big-gift revival will continue, at least for a small slice of the higher-education universe. "Big donors want big impact, and American research universities in particular can legitimately claim to deal with the large challenges faced by our society in the twenty-first century," the firm stated in a February 2014 special report.

With the potential for big donations growing, fundraising is a major activity for colleges, increasingly even at two-year institutions. Some big universities operate fundraising operations that employ hundreds of people. Much of their fundraising efforts are focused on alumni, who give about a quarter of all donations. According to the Council for Aid to Education, however, foundations still provide the biggest share of donations, (about 30 percent); nonalumni individual donors provide about 18 percent and corporations about 15 percent. Higher-education donors are also picky about how their money is spent. All but about 10 percent is given with the stipulation that it be used for a particular purpose.

As with endowments, the benefits of that philanthropy are spread unevenly across the higher-education landscape. In its analyses of college spending and revenues, the Delta Cost Project found that the combined effects of philanthropy and endowment returns paid off big for only certain kinds of the institutions. For the 2011 year, for example, revenue from gifts, investment returns, and endowment income amounted to more than $39,000 per full-time-equivalent student at private research institutions and more than $17,000 per student at private bachelor's institutions, but just $150 per student at community colleges.[11]

Don't most public colleges get the majority of their support from their states?

For more than one hundred years, that was the case. But following a decade of declines in state funding coupled with tuition increases, revenue from tuition now exceeds state and local funding at public research universities and public master's colleges, and tuition revenue is nearly equal to the amount of government funding that goes to public bachelor's colleges. Although state funding has certainly fallen, it does not necessarily mean schools have significantly less money; figures from the Delta Cost Project show that such institutions now receive more in net tuition on average than they lost in state support. The same is not true for community colleges, where state funding was also cut but tuition increases did not make up for the difference; on a per-student basis, these institutions have ended up with less money.[12]

Looking at this shift in state support another way, in twenty-four states in 2012, the share of revenue for public colleges coming from students through tuition and fees exceeded the share coming from the state. As recently as 2000, that had been the case in only three states.[13]

Why do people say states have "disinvested" in public higher education?

In one (small) sense, they have not. Except for small dips in 1992 and 1993, another in 2004, and then two big decreases during the worst years of the Great Recession, overall spending by states on higher education has increased every year for half a century. But state funding has not kept up with inflation or the significant growth in college enrollment. And as states have increased their spending on other programs and services, most notably on Medicaid, the share of state funds going to higher education has shrunk. In 1987, spending on higher education made up about 12 percent of state budgets and Medicaid about 10 percent. By 2011, higher education accounted for just about 10 percent and Medicaid nearly a quarter. Higher education was not singled out; the increased spending on Medicaid has also cut into the share of state budgets going to elementary and secondary schools, transportation, public assistance, and every other government service except corrections.[14] With states still facing rising costs for deferred maintenance of their roads and other infrastructure as well as unfunded pension liabilities, prospects for a major turnaround in higher-education funding are not great.

The cuts in state- and local-government spending that came in the wake of the 2008 financial crisis and the Great Recession were the most severe, and spurred the spike in public-college tuition prices that this country has seen in recent years. (States provide most of the public money to public colleges but localities also provide some support, mostly to community colleges.) Between 2007 and 2012 state and local appropriations to public colleges per full-time-equivalent student declined by 23 percent, even counting the federal "stimulus funding" that states put toward higher education. Fourteen states cut funding by 30 percent or more. The only states that increased spending on public colleges during this period were Illinois (mostly to make up for historically underfunded pensions, not for college operations), and North Dakota, where the state economy has been buoyed by an energy boom. By 2012 nationally, state and local spending per full-time-equivalent student fell to $6020, the lowest it has been in twenty-five years in inflation-adjusted terms. That is 24 percent below the pre-crash level of 2008 (and about 32 percent lower than the all-time high in 2001), according to State Higher Education Executives Officers.[15] In 2013, state and local support for higher education began to rebound, but even so, state and local spending per full-time-equivalent rose only modestly to $6105.[16]

Yet during the same period, between 2007 and 2012, the average sticker price for tuition at four-year public colleges increased by 27 percent, after accounting for inflation. Nearly a third of the states increased their tuition by more than that average, most notably California, which enrolls more public college students than any other state, and where sticker prices rose by more than 70 percent during this period.[17] In many states the tuition increases were often accompanied by layoffs, furloughs, hiring freezes, pay cuts, and caps on enrollment. While no one has done a comprehensive accounting of the cuts, one assessment, by the Center on Budget and Policy Priorities, found that colleges and universities in California, Arizona, Colorado, Louisiana, Nevada, New Hampshire, and North Carolina, were especially hard hit.[18] That was particularly true at the California Community Colleges, where enrollment caps shut out a half-million students between 2008 and 2012, a number equal to the total enrollment at the California State University System. In November 2012, California voters approved an increase in the sales tax that helped to restore some of the funding.

While students have assumed more of the burden for the cost of college from states, as will be discussed in further depth below, the burden of providing financial aid has also shifted, but in a slightly different way. As the number of low-income college students has grown, the federal government has increased its support for need-based aid, and now bears an even bigger share of those costs relative to the states than it did before. In 2008, for every $1000 worth of Pell Grants, states provided an additional $400 from their own need-based aid programs. By 2012, the level of federal spending had increased so that for every $1000 worth of Pell Grants, state funds accounted for about $210. It is not that the states have cut back. In fact, as the Pell Institute shows in an analysis, states' overall spending on need-based aid between 2008 and 2012 actually increased by 10 percent, in inflation-adjusted dollars, even as overall state support for higher education declined by about the same percentage. But while federal spending on Pell Grants more than tripled during this period, state funding for need-based aid did not even double.[19] In 2012, three states— Georgia, New Hampshire, and South Dakota—offered no student aid based purely on financial need. In another fifteen states fewer than one out of ten Pell Grant recipients received need-based aid from a state program.[20]

The divestment is disturbing to public-college leaders and others who fear that shrinking state support will cripple institutions, and student opportunity, for years to come. And a few have not been shy in saying so. At a time when economic growth is being driven by college-educated workers, Mortenson, of the Pell Institute, calls the record of decades-plus disinvestment by states "stunning and stupid."[21]

The decline in state funding also worries federal officials, who, as part of the next version of the Higher Education Act, are now eyeing student-aid policies that could encourage states to keep up their funding for higher education and perhaps punish those that do not. The Higher Education Act, which is slated for its next renewal in 2014 or 2015, is the legislation that sets the rules for Pell Grants, student loans, and dozens of other postsecondary-education programs funded and overseen by the federal government. Both President Obama and Secretary of Education Arne Duncan have criticized states for cuts in spending on higher education.

How have tuition prices changed over the past few decades?

College "sticker" prices have risen at more than three times the rate of inflation since 1971. (That is a figure that is often quoted, but here is the math: From 1971 to 2013, the inflation rate was 475 percent, and according to data from the College Board, the average sticker price at four-year private colleges increased by 1,543 percent, at four-year public colleges by more than 1,900 percent, and at community colleges by 1,600 percent.)

Annual increases in tuition prices were not always the norm. In the 1970s—the decade many parents of today's traditional-aged college students were themselves in school—public and private college tuition increases actually lagged behind the rate of inflation. In each of the decades since then, however, college prices have risen by at least twice the rate of inflation, except at community colleges in the 1990s, where prices stayed more in check.[22] Many experts pin 1985 as the start of this new era, a period marked by what University of Kentucky higher-education scholar John R. Thelin calls "an enduring pattern of cost escalation" that included increased spending on new residence halls, recreation centers, and other facilities, as well as on merit scholarships.[23] With the last of the baby boomers having gone through college by then, many of the institutions began spending in hopes of gaining a competitive edge as the pool of high-school students got smaller.

As many commentators have been quick to note in recent years, higher-education spending has increased faster than that of most other goods and services except for health insurance. A chart published by Bloomberg News in 2013 makes this abundantly clear. It shows that between 1985 and 2012, the price of college increased by 538 percent (whether public, private, or an average of both is not specified), compared to a 121-percent increase in the consumer-price index, a 286-percent increase in costs for medical care, and rise in housing costs of about 140 percent.[24]

Not so coincidently, 1985 was also the year *U.S. News & World Report* began annual publication of what is now the most influential rankings of America's colleges. As critics of *U.S. News* have noted, its rankings are heavily driven by factors that are tied directly to how much colleges spend. For example, by spending more on merit aid for top students, colleges can improve the academic profile of their student body, which helps them in the rankings. Many experts blame the influence of *U.S. News* for contributing to the rise of college costs, although of course, ultimately it is the colleges themselves that are responsible for their actions.

Some economists argue that comparing college prices with inflation or the price of housing is an imperfect measure. For one, the measure of inflation accounts for the costs of a broad range of goods and services, while higher-education is a service industry and one that is made up of many high-skilled employees. Moreover, as the authors Robert B. Archibald and David H. Feldman argue in *Why Does College Cost So Much,* the technological changes that have reshaped the American economy over the past century may have cut the costs for many manufactured products through labor-saving gains in productivity, but they have not lowered costs for the kinds of services provided by other high-skilled workers, including lawyers, accountants, and dentists. (Archibald and Feldman, both professors at the College of William & Mary, point out that the price of dental care increased at about the same rate as the price of college from 1947 to 2006.[25]) They do not say that colleges are particularly efficient, but they do contend that as long as higher education remains "artisan" in the way it educates students, favoring teaching through personal interactions with high-skilled personnel that is not mass produced, its costs will rise faster than those of many other sectors of the economy. This is one of the reasons so many of today's discussions about lowering college costs now focus on the idea of using distance education and other technology-enhanced tools to improve college "productivity."

So how expensive is college?

There is no simple answer to this question. Certainly, there are institutions that carry a high price tag. In the 2013–2014 academic year, 168 private colleges carried a sticker price of more than $50,000 a year for tuition, room, and board, up from 123 two years earlier. (Seven public institutions—the University of Michigan and six University of California campuses—are now priced that high too, for out-of-state students.) About 60 percent of the high-priced institutions are concentrated in four states that have traditionally been home to elite private colleges: California, Massachusetts, New York, and Pennsylvania.

Those five-digit prices are the numbers that typically draw the alarmist headlines. Yet in the same 2013–2014 school year, half of all four-year public-college students attended an institution where the in-state sticker price for tuition and fees was lower than $9,011, and 85 percent attended an institution where the fees were below $15,000. The average tuition at community colleges, which enroll about 40 percent of undergraduates, is $3,260. Private colleges, which enroll fewer than one in five undergraduates, cost more. But even in that sector, half of all four-year private-college students attended an institution where the sticker price for tuition and fees ran less than $31,290. Costs for food and housing, plus books and other expenses, add to that—on average about $14,000 worth at both public and private nonprofit four-year colleges. But at the same time, two-thirds of all full-time students do not actually pay the full sticker price because of scholarships and other financial aid.[26]

Is this why people talk about colleges having a "sticker price" and a "net price"?

Yes. Much of the debate over rising college prices focuses on the sticker price, but it is the "net price"—the price after deducting student aid—that ultimately determines college affordability. As with an airplane full of passengers where every person on the flight might be paying a different fare, different students at a college might be paying a different "net price," depending on the amount of aid they are awarded.

Unfortunately, there is not even a commonly accepted definition of "net price." The two entities with the best access to college-price data and the most visible reports—the College Board and the Department of Education—each calculate it differently. (The College Board counts things like the value of tax credits and tax deductions but only measures full-time students; the Education Department, on its student-focused College Navigator site, calculates net price only for first-time, full-time freshman and does not factor in the tax benefits.) Most analysts use the College Board data because it covers more students, even though its calculation of net tuition— by counting tax breaks—seems to portray colleges in a more favorable light on matters of net tuition increases.

Sticker prices for private and public colleges rose sharply in the past two decades—they more than doubled since 1993 at four-year public colleges even after accounting for inflation—but net prices have not risen nearly as fast, according to the College Board. That is because overall levels of student aid have increased as well.

In 2013–2014, the average sticker price at a four-year private college was $30,090, up 69 percent after inflation from the price in 1993–1994. But the average net price of $12,460 was only about 22 percent higher. The average sticker price at a four-year public college was $8,890, up 117 percent even after inflation, in part reflecting the big hikes in tuition that many public colleges instituted to make up for cuts in state support that began with the Great Recession. The average net price of $3,120 at public-four-year colleges represented a 53-percent increase. And at community colleges, while the average sticker price of $3,260 was 62 percent higher than in 1993, the average net price as calculated by the College Board actually fell by several hundred percent. That was because the tuition at those institutions was still relatively low, and because so many of their students were so poor that the Pell Grants and other aid they received far exceeded the price of tuition.[27]

Undergraduate student aid of all forms (grant, loans, work-study funds, and tax credits) and from all sources (the federal and state governments and institutions themselves) added up to more than $185 billion in 2012–2013, a fourfold increase over the level twenty years earlier after adjusting for inflation, according to the College Board's estimates. Loans increased by the biggest amount during the same twenty-year period but spending on federal grants and institutional aid more than tripled, and state aid nearly did as well. In total, the College Board estimates students received more than $45 billion in Pell Grants and veterans and military benefits, nearly $35 billion in aid from colleges themselves, and more than $9.5 billion in merit and need-based aid from states.

Notably, the value of federal tax credits and deductions, which benefit wealthier families and were nonexistent twenty years ago, amounted to nearly $17 billion in 2013. More students benefit from the tax breaks than do those who receive Pell Grants, although the value of the benefit is typically smaller.[28] (The figures on federal spending do not include graduate-student aid.)

During the same twenty-year period that these levels of aid were rising, however, the number of undergraduates increased by about 46 percent. And while college prices were rising substantially higher than inflation during the past two decades, family incomes were not. The median family income in 2012 was $51,017, barely 4 percent higher than what it was twenty years earlier in inflation-adjusted dollars. So even though the increases in aid were substantial, their effect on affordability was limited by the boom in enrollments and the near-invisible increase in family incomes. The federal government more than doubled the size of the maximum Pell Grant between 1995 and 2013—bringing it from $2,340 to $5,645—but even with that increase, the maximum grant covers less than two-thirds of the average sticker price for tuition and room, and board at a four-year public college. And not everyone gets the full amount; the average Pell Grant is about 65 percent of the maximum.

Figure 2.1 illustrates the conundrum. Tuition prices, both "net" and "sticker," have been rising steadily year after year for two decades, while many family incomes have stagnated.

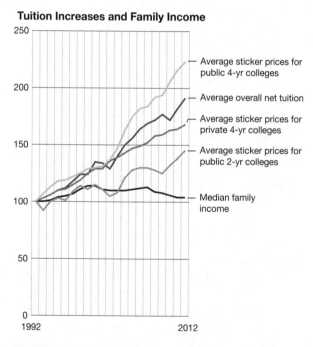

Figure 2.1 Tuition Increases and Family Income

Note: Data for median family income from the U.S. Census Bureau and The Parthenon Group; data for all other categories from "College Board Trends in College Pricing" by College Board and The Parthenon Group. Net tuition is the enrollment-weighted average across all sectors. All figures based on 2012 inflation-adjusted dollars.

Don't middle-class and even upper-income families struggle to pay for college, too?

Everyone thinks college is too expensive. And while it is true that wealthier families pay less of their income toward college expenses than poorer ones and can more easily take advantage of federal income-tax credits (families with incomes of as much as $180,000 can use the credits), for many such families, putting children through college can still be a major financial strain. That is one reason that college experts increasingly counsel students to broaden their search criteria and consider worthy but slightly less-selective colleges, where their academic or extracurricular record might be more likely to earn them a merit scholarship. "Nobody has to go broke," says Peter Van Buskirk, an admissions dean-turned-consultant. "A lot of it rests on the willingness of families to research the best fit."[29]

According to Department of Education data, in 2011–2012 students from higher-income families were more likely to win scholarships from outside sources and to be awarded merit aid from colleges too, compared with those from families earning below $50,000. Yet with tuition prices as high as they are today, even high-earning families can also sometimes qualify for need-based financial aid from colleges, particularly if they have more than one child in college at a time. In 2011–2012 about a quarter of all students from families with incomes over $50,000 a year received such aid, and 11 percent of families with incomes over $100,000 did so.[30]

The amount of need-based aid a student receives from a college depends on two factors. One is the "expected family contribution," or EFC, a calculation based largely on the family's annual income and the number of children in college. The other is the "cost of attendance," which includes things like textbooks and travel in addition to the college's tuition and room and board. That is why students who attend higher-priced colleges sometimes get more in aid than they would at lower-cost college. To calculate the EFC, most colleges use the methodology from the FAFSA form—which, to the benefit of wealthier applicants, does not count a family's home equity on their primary residence, nor retirement savings, nor assets tied up in a family-owned business with fewer than one hundred employees. The FAFSA methodology does take into account other family assets, but only above a certain amount and even then only counts on less than 6 percent of the value of parents' assets (and 20 percent of the student's) in determining the EFC.

.About four hundred colleges, mostly private, selective ones, use a different methodology to determine the EFC, which takes more of the family assets into account, making it a little harder for wealthier families to qualify for need-based aid from colleges. Although these alternative EFC calculations could in some circumstances appear to "punish" a family with a lot in savings, that would only be the case for the richest of families. The rest will be better off if they've been able to save, particularly because even coming up with the money to meet the EFC may tax some families. Also, many colleges may choose not to provide enough in financial aid to close the gap between the EFC and the cost of attendance—something financial-aid offices call "gapping" a student—making such savings critical for covering the remainder.

Half of all families with a child under the age of eighteen today have begun saving for their college expenses, according to the latest "How America Saves for College, 2014" report. That is down from 62 percent prior to the recession. Of those families, the average amount saved was a little over $15,000. The nonsavers, even those earning more than $100,000 a year, said the main reason they had not saved was that they did not have enough money to do so.

In the past, students would work their way through school. Why can't they just do that today?

Most students do work while attending college today. But to cover their costs, the combination of low wages and rising college prices would make for a very exhausting, and frankly unrealistic, work week. According to an analysis prepared by Mortenson, at the Pell Institute, an undergraduate at a minimum-wage job would have to work sixty-one hours a week for fifty-two weeks to earn enough to cover the $21,611 average cost of attendance at a four-year public college in 2012. In 1980, a student could have covered costs of attendance with twenty-one hours of work a week. A community college student would have to work thirty-seven hours to cover the cost of attendance in 2012. In 1980 it required nineteen hours to do so.[31]

How big is the student-loan burden?

At some point in late 2011, the total amount of outstanding student debt hit $1-trillion, more than the total that Americans had borrowed for cars and more than the debt on their credit cards. By 2012 the scary-sounding figure had become one of the most cited discussion points in the ongoing debate over the cost and value of college.

Some college critics say the availability of loans allows colleges to raise prices with impunity—an argument that has become known as the "Bennett hypothesis" because Bennett, the former U.S. secretary of education, is one of the most prominent figures in this camp. But many economists still maintain that student debt, for the most part, is "good debt" because students and society benefit from higher education. Recently, however, as this debt burden has grown ever larger, even some college advocates have begun sounding alarms about the long-term ramifications of rising student debt and the ways it could impair young adults' ability to buy a home or begin saving for retirement. Today four out of ten households headed by someone younger than thirty-five have student debt, according to a study by researchers at the University of Kansas.

Across all age groups combined, about 40 million Americans have student-loan debt, at a total value of more than $1.2 trillion—triple the level of 2004. The amount includes more than $1 trillion in federal student loans and around $200 billion in so-called private loans, which come from banks and other entities.

Those cumulative numbers are striking. But it is important to note that many other considerations are often overlooked in frenzy around student debt. For one, more students are going to college today than were in 2004, and the nation experienced a severe financial crisis during this period which forced more families to borrow. Also a lot of that growth in debt has come in the post-baccalaureate sector, where students borrow about three times as much annually as they do for undergraduate education and in the for-profit-college sector, which was expanding during most of this period. Recent reports estimate that about 40 percent of that $1 trillion-plus in student debt is attributable to students in graduate and professional programs.[32]

Still, according to the College Board, the average amount in federal student loans borrowed in the 2012–2013 academic year by undergraduates was $6760, compared to $5910 a decade earlier in inflation-adjusted dollars, while the average amount borrowed in the federal loan system by graduate students, $17,230, was nearly $2000 smaller than it was ten years earlier.[33]

Of course, students do not just borrow for one year. Typically undergraduates borrow for four (or more) years and sometimes from sources that are not part of the federal student-loan system. The latest report from the Project on Student Debt, which looks only at students graduating from four-year colleges, found that seven out of ten seniors who graduated in 2012 had borrowed to attend college, and were leaving college with an average debt of $29,400—about one-fifth of which was in private loans. Private loans carry fewer protections and repayment options than federal student loans and often carry higher interest rates.

The national average is inflated by the students at for-profit colleges. For-profit college students borrow at higher rates (88 percent) than students at public colleges (66 percent), or private nonprofit colleges (75 percent), and they borrow more money. The average debt for a student graduating from a four-year for-profit college was $39,950, compared to $32,300 at nonprofit colleges and $25,500 at public colleges. For-profit-college students are also more likely to have borrowed through a private loan once they've hit the borrowing limit on federal student loans, because their colleges typically do not offer as much in financial aid as public and private nonprofit colleges and because more of them are independent students and therefore cannot rely on federal Parent Plus loans. Nationally 30 percent of graduating students had a private loan, but among for-profit college students, 41 percent did.[34]

Borrowing by students at two-year colleges is a newer phenomenon. Until the turn of this century, only about 5 percent of community college students took out loans for school, and those who did borrowed less than $2,500 a year, on average. But over the past decade-plus, as tuition costs rose and general economic conditions worsened, borrowing by community-college students has increased. As of 2012, more than 16 percent of those students borrow an average of more than $4,500 a year.[35]

The colleges where students graduate with the most debt are not necessarily those that charge the highest prices. Part of the reason for this is because some high-priced institutions also offer more in student aid to make up the difference; additionally, many such institutions simply enroll fewer students who need to borrow. For the thousand or so individual colleges that reported their average debt levels, the Project on Student debt found 122 where the average student debt was greater than $35,000. Averages, however, can give a distorted picture, as can anecdotal accounts of individuals struggling with six-figure debt. As the College Board in 2013 reported, 40 percent of the student debt is for balances of less than

$10,000 and 70 percent is for less than $25,000. Only about 4 percent of all borrowers, including those who have borrowed for law, business, and medical school, have debt balances above $100,000.

Still, even the average debt carried by graduates of public and nonprofit four-year colleges can present a formidable financial challenge for borrowers in the current economy. Based on the 2014–2015 unsubsidized interest rates for government loans and a typical ten-year repayment schedule, a graduate would need to pay about $330 a month to pay off the average college graduate's loan balance.[36] Assuming borrowers devote 10 percent of gross pay toward repaying the loan, they would need an annual salary of more than $39,540 to repay the loan without facing economic hardship. (For a subsidized loan, available to those who qualify based on financial need, the monthly payment would be $307.) The difficult job market has left many recent graduates unable to land positions with salaries at that level, which adds to the growing national anxiety over student debt.

This anxiety is not only focused on young people, either. According to the Federal Reserve, Americans aged sixty and over owe more than $43 billion in student loans, and the number of borrowers of that age group is at an all-time high of 2.2 million. Some of this is debt taken on for other family members, but some is also their own.[37]

One politically sensitive aspect of the student-debt problem concerns students who take out more in student loans than they need for college and related expenses, either to help out their families who need the money or simply because they can. While the size of this borrowing is unknown, some colleges and student-lending experts have begun talking more openly about ways of limiting what they call "excess student borrowing." Student advocates note, however, that for some of these students, borrowing for such purposes is legal and for some, may serve as a necessary social safety net.

What steps are being taken to address this debt burden?

There are many organizations and individuals who are working to bring about broader understanding of the economic impact of students carrying student-loan debt into their working lives, in the hopes that such understanding will lead to alternative approaches to financing college. These groups worry that the burden will exacerbate a "wealth gap" that could keep young people from buying homes and saving for retirement, and perhaps even have an intergenerational effect if it ultimately makes it harder for them to send their own children to college.[38] Various research groups, along with organizations like Opportunity Nation, advocate for federally funded Children's Savings Accounts to replace or augment the existing reliance on student loans.

Other groups have been pushing for changes to overhaul the student-loan repayment system to make it even easier for borrowers to use income-contingent payment plans, as is the practice in Australia and other countries. One such proposal comes from the University of Michigan's Dynarski and one of her colleagues there, Daniel Kreisman, who argue that the issue with student loans and the standard ten-year repayment plan is not so much a debt crisis but "a repayment crisis." The problem, they say, is caused by a system developed back when students were not borrowing as much and that currently requires them to start repaying these larger loans when they are beginning their careers and not making much money. They say loan pay-off periods should run as long as twenty-five years "to reflect the decades of increased earnings that education produces." [39] Others worry that the prospect of such a long repayment period could deter students who should be borrowing from doing so.

Students and recent college graduates themselves have also mobilized to publicize debt issues and lobby for more-forgiving repayment options, most visibly through an organization called Young Invincibles, and a more ad hoc group called Student Debt Crisis. Young Invincibles, founded in 2009, began as an advocacy organization for young people in the debates over health care reform. Student Debt Crisis was co-founded the same year by a New York City lawyer named Robert Applebaum, who in 2009—amid bailouts of big Wall Street banks in the news—gained notoriety with a campaign and petition drive that called on the government to forgive student loan debt. In 2011 the Obama Administration opened up more income-based repayment options for borrowers, and government officials credited the petition drive for helping to spur the move.

In 2013, after heated debate over the degree to which government should subsidize student borrowing or let rates on student loans more closely reflect market conditions, Congress set the interest rate on subsidized federal student loans at 3.8 percent (close to the historically low rate that was current at the time), and agreed that it would be re-set each year based on the yield of the ten-year Treasury note, with maximum rate of 8.5 percent.[40]

The federal government now offers four loan-repayment plans designed to ease the debt burden by allowing borrowers to pay off their loans through payments based on their income and, in some cases, have portions of those loans eventually forgiven. But the eligibility rules can be confusing, and only a small portion of borrowers use them.

Which sectors produce the highest rates of student-loan defaults?

Students at for-profit colleges default at higher rates than those at public and nonprofit colleges. According to the most recent U.S. Department of Education calculation, 21.8 percent of for-profit-college students defaulted within three years of when they were to begin repaying their loans, higher than the national average default rate for all students of 14.7 percent. The default rate for students at four-year public colleges was 13 percent, and for private nonprofit-college students it was 8.2 percent. Within the public-college sector, the default rate for community colleges was higher—20.9 percent—although the number of community college students who borrow is low. By contrast, for-profit college students accounted for nearly a third of the four million borrowers who were due to begin repaying their student loans in the 2010 fiscal year—disproportionately greater than their share of the overall student population because of their higher rates of borrowing—and they accounted for 46 percent of all defaults.

What is the significance of a default rate?

The default rate is an indicator of the difficulty borrowers are having in repaying their loans, but it also has an impact on colleges. Whether they have graduated or not, borrowers are required to begin repaying their loans six months after leaving college. Each year the U.S. Department of Education counts the number of students from each college who entered repayment status and then tracks them as a cohort for up to three years. It then calculates an official "cohort default rate" for every college that participates in federal student-aid programs. (The department used to track borrowers for just two years but under a 2011 change in the law, it began tracking them for three, and beginning in 2014, the three-year rate is the official rate by which colleges are judged.) Institutions with rates above certain thresholds could be barred from participating in federal student aid programs. While this cut-off from student aid based on default rates is ostensibly one of the government's most important tools for holding colleges accountable for preparing students to succeed well enough to pay off their loans, in reality, few colleges are ever cut off. This is true for two reasons: first, because the thresholds are so high, and second, because some colleges employ "default management" strategies, such as encouraging borrowers most at risk of defaulting to obtain loan deferments or forbearances, which keeps a potential default out of the calculation.

The for-profit-college industry argues, correctly, that its students are among the most economically disadvantaged. Claiming that this makes such students more likely to default, it has pushed for measures that would provide higher default-rate thresholds for enrolling such students. But critics of the sector note the high default rates are a sign that some colleges are victimizing students who are often unsophisticated about college and the risks for debt. In some instances colleges have recruited students into expensive programs for which they were not qualified, or into programs that are not properly accredited, leaving borrowers unable to qualify for jobs in those fields when they graduate and therefore harder-pressed to repay their loans.

What is the difference between the price and the cost of college?

As we have seen, price (be it the published price or the net price) is the amount colleges charge students to attend. Cost is the amount they spend to provide education. Price and cost are of course related, but colleges that have the authority to set their tuition prices (not all public universities do) often set their prices based on other factors besides their actual costs, including market forces like prices that their competitors are charging. Colleges that price themselves at the high end of the spectrum are said to be pursuing the "Chivas Regal" effect, based on the apparently apocryphal story that the scotch became more desirable after it was priced higher. (The reality is that the popularity grew as the scotch company also boosted its marketing, so the analogy to higher education, where marketing has also become more prevalent, may be even more apt.) The previously discussed "Bennett hypothesis," which has gained popular currency in recent years as commentators analogize the housing bubble, fed by easier-to-get-mortgages, with the so-called higher-education bubble, fed by easier-to-get student loans, also may play a role in colleges' pricing decisions.

Trends on college costs are harder to track and analyze than college prices because college budgets are complex and the available data have not been kept as consistently. But according to one analysis that looks only at expenditures for educational costs, spending per student in the public sector increased by about 25 percent over four decades ending in 2010, even after adjusting for inflation. The pattern of that spending, however, was not steady. It was relatively flat from 1970 to 1985, flat again in the early 1990s, and declined by about 10 percent in the decade ending in 2010, at which point the per-student spending was about at the same level as it was in 1995. Some of the declines in per-student spending came because the overall spending did not keep up with the growth in enrollments. At private colleges, spending per student actually fell in the 1970s, but then roughly doubled after that. In the thirty years between 1980 and 2010, spending per student increased in "fits and starts," but tuition and fees increased consistently, says Hauptman, the policy consultant and expert on college finances who did the analysis.[41]

All colleges thus became more dependent on tuition as a revenue source during this period. Especially for public colleges, where government funds had historically been the main source of support (along with grants and gifts), this represents a significant change. At public colleges, tuition and fees accounted for 18 percent of what colleges spent per student in 1980 but climbed to 40 percent by 2010. (College finance experts often use data based on spending per student when writing about college costs to better compare institutions of different sizes or make comparisons that adjust for enrollment growth over time.) At private colleges, tuition and fees accounted for 45 percent of what colleges spent per student in 1980 but 52 percent by 2010.[42] Yet, as we have discussed, even with tuition as high as it, it generally covers just a portion of the actual costs of a college education even at private universities.

Just as there are theories about why college prices rise, so too are there theories about the causes of rising costs. One, which relates to the previously mentioned work by Archibald and Feldman at William & Mary, is known as "cost disease," a term coined by economists William Baumol and William Bowen in the 1960s. They used it to explain cost escalation in certain labor-intensive industries like health care, higher education, and the arts, where the "quality of the labor required to produce these services is difficult to reduce."[43] The theory is often illustrated by noting that a string quartet playing a one-minute waltz will always require four musicians and sixty seconds. Under that theory, higher-education is the equivalent of that labor-intensive waltz. The rest of the theory posits that productivity gains elsewhere will raise overall earnings, so that labor-intensive services where costs do not fall—including concerts and college—nonetheless still remain generally affordable. But as we have seen, many families have not enjoyed earnings growth since the late 1990s. (In 2013, median family income was below the 1997 level, in inflation-adjusted terms.)

The second major theory, known as "Bowen's Law," comes courtesy of the economist Howard Bowen, who argued in 1981 that colleges, in pursuit of better students, better faculty, better facilities, and other traditional measures of prestige, will raise as much money as they can and then spend all that they raise. Ronald G. Ehrenberg, a Cornell University economist and himself an expert on college costs, likens this to the Sesame Street character Cookie Monster and his never-ending quest for chocolate-chip sweets.

Are the factors that drive prices at private nonprofit colleges different from those at public institutions? What about for-profit colleges?

Many of the factors that drive prices, and costs, at various kinds of institutions are the same—salaries, new facilities, investments in technology, the addition of new services for students like more counseling. But the increases in tuition and fees at public colleges over the past several years have come in response to steep cuts in state support and, to the degree that costs do drive prices, perhaps in response to rising expenses for health-care benefits for employees. At private nonprofit colleges, higher prices appear to be spurred by bigger outlays for scholarships, both those based on students' financial need and merit aid, which, at institutions lacking large endowments is essentially a "tuition discount" for some students and a cost to others.

For-profit colleges operate on a different model. For one, their price is based on the need to turn a profit, and until the recent downturn in for-profit-college enrollment, most were boasting profit margins of 15 to 30 percent. (Public and private nonprofit colleges, of course, aim to spend less than they take in too, but their surpluses rarely if ever hit such high margins.) Because so many for-profit college students are dependent on federal student-aid programs, many of the college companies also set their prices with an eye on the size of Pell Grants and student-loan limits, some years even raising their prices when the government raises the limit on how much a student can borrow to take advantage of students' higher borrowing options. Historically, the colleges have tended to set their prices above what public colleges charge and below typical charges of private colleges—the cost for a bachelor's degree in accounting at DeVry, for example, is about $17,150 a year. To combat steep declines in enrollments, however, many of the institutions in the past two years began advertising discounts and scholarships to attract students.

For-profit colleges also have to abide by a law known as the 90:10 rule, which prohibits them from receiving more than 90 percent of their revenues from federal student-aid programs such as Pell Grants and loans. Money from other federally funded programs, like GI Bill benefits, does not count in that 90 percent. Most of the biggest for-profit companies receive more than 80 percent of their revenues from federal-student aid programs, up from the 60-percent range a decade ago. The for-profit college industry argues that the 90:10 rule forces them to raise their prices. (In a move that student advocates called "the height of cynicism," one company close to exceeding that 90 percent threshold, Corinthian Colleges Inc., deliberately raised tuition rates at several of its colleges higher than the combined Pell Grant and loan maximum in 2011, to ensure that it would be receiving revenue from sources other than Pell Grants and federal loans—forcing some students to borrow even more via private loans—so it could avoid violating the 90:10 rule.) But student advocacy groups say some colleges deliberately recruit needy students—some of whom may lack sophistication about how to choose a college—because they know such students will qualify for Pell Grants and subsidized loans to pay. The advocates contend that the colleges could avoid hitting the 90-percent cap if they offered better programs at more affordable prices, so a bigger proportion of their student body and revenues came from, for example, students paying through their employers' tuition-assistance programs. Some for-profit colleges have recently altered their recruiting tactics to try to enroll such students.

A proposed and controversial new federal rule, known as the "gainful employment" regulation, which would apply to all for-profit colleges as well as some programs at community colleges and other institutions, is seen by some colleges as an indirect attempt at price control. The Education Department regulation would cut off financial-aid eligibility for programs if too many of its graduates end up earning too little relative to their student debt, thereby creating an incentive for colleges to keep the prices of their programs from getting too expensive. As proposed the rule would apply only to certain career-focused programs at nonprofit and public colleges, but some officials in those sectors worry that the concept could eventually be applied more broadly across higher education.

What is a "discount rate," and why is the rise in this rate a concern?

Colleges do not boast about their discount rates on their web sites or their marketing brochures, but they are an important measure of a college's financial health. And over the past several years, those measures have been pointing to weakening bottom lines. The discount rate measures the proportion of revenue that would have been generated as income to the college based on the sticker price that is instead diverted for scholarships, grants, and other forms of student aid. For example, if a college's sticker price is $35,000 and the institution could enroll one thousand students at that price, it would have $35 million in tuition revenue and a discount rate of zero. But almost no college is in that position. Instead, as we have seen, colleges set a sticker price hoping that some students will pay it, and then offer need-based and merit scholarships to students who might be reluctant or unable to afford to attend at that price but would at a lower price. The proportional difference between the $35 million and the amount in tuition that ends up in the college's coffers (its net tuition) is its discount rate. Some colleges also use donations or earnings from their endowments to provide scholarships. That spending does not cut into tuition-revenue expectations but is often counted in the discount-rate calculations.

Tuition discounting is not new, but it has become more prevalent, even at public colleges, with the increasing competition for students and the proliferation of enrollment-management consultants boasting of sophisticated formulas on how much to award to which student. That expertise notwithstanding, tuition discounting has also become more costly and some analysts contend that colleges are discounting themselves into financial trouble. According to the latest annual survey by the National Association of College and University Business Officers, which included results from 401 private colleges, institutions discounted tuition by an estimated average of 41 percent overall and more than 46 percent for freshmen in

2013–14. That is a lot of foregone revenue. And even with those all-time high discount rates, many of the colleges still reported fall-offs in enrollment. The enrollment losses were particularly acute among the four-year colleges with fewer than four thousand students, the kinds of institutions that are generally thought to be the most vulnerable as students are becoming more price conscious. The head of the biggest private college association estimates that only about a quarter of all students at private colleges pay the full price, and at some less-competitive colleges, fewer than one out of ten do.

More worrisome still for many colleges, signs suggest that there is little relief in sight. A survey by Moody's Investors Service in fall 2013 found tuition concerns even among the four-year public colleges whose debt it rates. (Bond ratings are only given to organizations that pay to get them, and typically those are the ones with strong enough finances to issue debt on the public market.) Of the 114 respondents, 28 percent said they expected declines in net tuition in the coming years and 44 percent reported that the increases in net-tuition revenue that they did expect would not keep up with inflation. According to Moody's, it has been two decades since the prospects for tuition-revenue growth have been this poor.

Some of this pressure to keep tuition revenue in check comes from the states themselves. In 2013, for example, Iowa lawmakers voted to freeze in-state tuition for the year at the state's three public universities and passed a law that prohibits them from using tuition revenues from in-state students to pay for financial aid. Likewise in California, where voters approved a sales-tax increase in 2012, Governor Jerry Brown has proposed budgets requiring tuition freezes at the University of California and California State University systems for a total of four years in return for their receiving additional state support.

Recently private colleges like Ashland University in Ohio, Concordia University in Minnesota, Converse College in South Carolina, and Wilson College in Pennsylvania, have tried to upend this "high-tuition, high-discount" model by announcing major price cuts. The institutions are betting that the steps will appeal to students and yield the same levels of net-tuition revenue as they were getting under the other strategy. As William M. Webster IV, a Converse trustee, explained to *The Chronicle of Higher Education* after the women's college announced plans to slash its sticker price by 43 percent to $16,500, the high-tuition, high-aid model "becomes more and more difficult to execute the further up the tuition-discount scale you go."[44]

Are some colleges in such financial trouble that they are in danger of closing, merging, or being acquired?

It is hard to kill a college, but since the turn of this century, several dozen have succumbed to financial pressures. According to the Department of Education's 2012 Digest of Education Statistics, fifty-seven degree-granting four-year colleges or branches, many of them small and religiously focused, closed their doors between 2000 and late 2012, along with eleven private two-year colleges. Nearly a hundred for-profit colleges closed as well during this period. The shuttered nonprofits include institutions like Mount Scenario College in Wisconsin, which closed in 2002, Dana College in Nebraska, which closed in 2010, and Lambuth University in Tennessee, which shut down in 2011. Since then several more have closed, including St. Paul's College in Virginia, which closed its doors in the summer of 2013 after failing to complete a merger with another historically black institution in North Carolina. And a few others took part in mergers, including public colleges in Georgia where, in 2013, the state consolidated eight public institutions into four to save money, and in Washington State, where City University of Seattle, a private college, became affiliated with the National University System.

In the wake of the closing of St. Paul's, which in its last semester had only about one hundred students, analysts from

Moody's warned that other colleges with tiny enrollments and "a high reliance on student charges, indistinct market positions, and limited donor support," were also at financial risk. "We anticipate more closures for these types of colleges given the current pressures on all higher-education revenue sources and increased accreditation scrutiny," Moody's analysts said, while also noting that these colleges make up a "small subset" of higher education.

That Education Department's tally of closed institutions, however, does not tell the whole story. It does not include institutions like Waldorf College in Iowa or Kendall College in Illinois, which were taken over by private companies and now operate as for-profit colleges. Kendall is part of Laureate Education, a company that owns or operates some seventy colleges and universities around the world. Nor does it include two small financially floundering religious colleges, Grand Canyon University in Arizona and Franciscan University of the Prairies in Iowa, each of which, after being acquired by investors in the mid-2000s, became ground-based campuses for fast-growing publicly traded for-profit college companies with tens of thousands of online students each. The Iowa campus, renamed Ashford University, is owed by Bridgepoint Education Inc. Grand Canyon is owned by Grand Canyon Education Inc. In the mid-2000s, the acquisition of financially ailing nonprofit colleges by for-profit investors seemed likely to become a small trend. But the practice has slowed in recent years—in part because accreditors have taken a harder line on the tactic.

Many colleges that have not closed continue to face financial strains. A survey of more than four hundred private colleges and regional state universities by *The Chronicle of Higher Education* in fall of 2013 found that nearly half had missed their enrollment or net-tuition goals for that year.[45] And in 2013 and 2014 at least a dozen private colleges, most of them small and located in parts of the country where numbers of traditional-aged students are shrinking, instituted layoffs and program closures in the wake of falling enrollments, according to *Inside Higher Ed.*[46] One of them, Iowa Wesleyan, a college of about six hundred students, eliminated sixteen of its thirty-two majors, including history and sociology, and made plans to lay off nearly half of its fifty faculty members and nearly a quarter of its seventy-eight staff members.[47]

Do for-profit colleges pose a competitive threat to traditional colleges and universities?

It is hard to find a higher-education topic that evokes more passion than the for-profit-colleges industry. Industry leaders and its defenders paint it as a crucial element of the national efforts to educate more Americans, particularly low-income and minority students who are not attending public and nonprofit colleges.

The industry also portrays itself as the "tax-paying" rather than tax-supported arm of higher education, a premise that its critics find fatuous considering that many for-profit colleges have geared their entire business model around students who pay with Pell Grants, federal student loans, and federal military and veterans' benefits.

In their early incarnations—back before institutions like the University of Phoenix in the late 1970s began offering baccalaureate degrees—most for-profit colleges focused more on career-oriented programs in business, health care, and trades. Many still operate in those realms, offering certificate and degree programs in fields like medical assisting, culinary arts, and HVAC and automotive repair. That puts those kinds of for-profits more in competition with community colleges, which for the most part offer associate degree and nondegree programs, than with traditional four-year baccalaureate colleges.

Although for-profits are pricier, they often win students based on their more-convenient scheduling; only the biggest community colleges, for example, enroll and start students year round the way many for-profit institutions do. For-profit colleges now award nearly half of all vocational certificates issued by educational institutions—credentials which can help recipients improve their salary prospects in less time than it takes to get a two- or four-year degree. The big caveats: for-profit colleges charge on average three times as much as community colleges for certificate programs and credentials in some fields can be a waste of money because they do not lead to higher earnings.[48])

Beginning in the 1990s, however, more for-profit colleges began expanding into the baccalaureate and advanced-degree market, and while those institutions make up just a small share of the for-profit universe, they now dominate in for-profit-college enrollments. About two-thirds of all students at for-profit colleges attend institutions offering four-year degrees and above. As mentioned, many of these institutions are owned by companies whose stock is traded on Wall Street or by giant private investment funds. Besides the University of Phoenix, owned by Apollo Education Group, these include: Ashford, owned by Bridgepoint,: American InterContinental University, owned by Career Education Corporation; Argosy University, owned by Education Management Corporation; Capella University, owned by Capella Education Inc.; DeVry University, owned by DeVry Education Group; Grand Canyon, owned by Grand Canyon Education Inc.; Kaplan University, formerly owned by the Washington Post Company and now by Graham Holdings; Walden University, owned by Laureate; and Westwood University, owned by Alta Colleges Inc. (Many of the parent companies also own other colleges; DeVry, for example, owns Chamberlain College of Nursing and several medical institutions in Latin America, while Education Management owns a chain of art and culinary schools known as the Art Institutes.)

These institutions were also among the first to capitalize on distance-education after the mid-1990s, and used their online advantage to attract "nontraditional" students for their undergraduate programs and to establish a stronghold in the market for master's degrees (and in the case of Phoenix,

Argosy, and Capella, even doctoral-level degrees) in fields like business, education, and information technology. In 2006 the Department of Education eliminated a regulation that restricted the growth of distance education. The regulation formerly allowed federal student loans and grants to be used only at colleges where distance-education students made up less than half the enrollments. When that restriction was lifted, for-profits were well-positioned to expand their online operations even further.

As for-profit college enrollments swelled, so too did their share of federal student aid and other federal funding. In 2011–2012, the latest year for which Department of Education data are available, nearly one out of every four dollars in Pell Grant funds were being spent at a for-profit college, up from 14 percent a decade earlier. Also that year, six of the top ten recipients of the military "tuition assistance" funds, which are available to active-duty service members, were for-profit colleges. The colleges also have attracted a disproportionately high share of veterans' GI Bill dollars, receiving 37 percent of the more than $4.4 billion spent from 2009 through 2011.[49]

The share of federal money going to for-profits, particularly the military benefits, has alarmed some student advocates and members of Congress who worry that taxpayer money is being used to fatten the profits of college companies that may not be providing useful educations to students. In the past few years, however, the for-profit industry has been losing ground amid a rash of media and government reports describing abusive practices by some for-profit colleges—many of them documented in a thousand-plus page report on thirty college companies compiled by U.S. Senator Tom Harkin (D-Iowa) in 2012. The Harkin Report came after a two-year investigation, and has been echoed by other inquiries, including, more recently, probes by a task force of state attorneys general and the federal Consumer Finance Protection Board. Together the investigations have brought to light cases of overly aggressive recruiting by admissions counselors trained to use a "pain funnel" approach to find applicants' vulnerabilities, falsification of job-placement data, rapacious pricing strategies, and deliberate obfuscation about costs and accreditation. Industry leaders maintain that such practices were not widespread and are largely in the past, and that the scrutiny is driven by ideological and political dislike of "for-profit" education. But critics of the sector contend that it has thrived by taking advantage of unsophisticated students leaving them with worthless degrees and student-loan debts they cannot afford to pay off.

Public and private nonprofit colleges, who have been developing their own online degree offerings and improving their marketing, are beginning to gain ground on for-profits. For example, the University of South Carolina's all-online Palmetto College, aimed at working adults who cannot relocate to complete their degrees, was created in 2013 specifically to win back market share from for-profit colleges in the state. Some public and private universities have even begun emphasizing the phrase "nonprofit" in their advertising on television spots and other media.

Does distance education make money for colleges?

Distance education—where students do not have to be physically present in the classroom—certainly can make money for colleges. But that is the case not necessarily because the course is online, but because of the way the many colleges have chosen to structure their distance-education operations. Those colleges that rely more heavily on adjuncts (whom they pay less than their own full-time faculty); run larger classes (since they are not limited by the size of a classroom); and use standardized courses (which saves on course-development costs) can be especially profitable, analysts say. Since most distance education courses are offered as online courses, the terms are generally used interchangeably, although it should be noted that not every distance-education student is an online student; some may be students who participate with other technologies or in low-residency or credit-by-exam programs.

Many nonprofit colleges work with outside companies to help them to create, market, and deliver their online programs, and under those arrangements, they often share the revenues with the companies on a fifty-fifty split. Among those partners are Pearson (a publishing company that bulked up its distance-education capacity in 2012 with a $650-million purchase of a company called Embanet); John Wiley & Sons (another publisher that bought the distance-education company Deltak for $220 million the same year), as well as companies called Bisk, Learning House, Academic Partnerships, and 2U. Whether in partnerships or with their own resources, some colleges have created thriving and profitable distance education operations that enroll far more students than they have on their campuses. These include institutions like Bellevue University in Nebraska, and Indiana Wesleyan and Southern New Hampshire Universities.

Do projected changes in the population of the country pose a threat to colleges' financial health?

From a demographic standpoint, colleges are in for a difficult decade, particularly those that cater to traditional-aged students. As the Western Interstate Commission for Higher Education has noted, the seventeen-year run of continuous growth in the number of high-school graduates ended in the spring of 2011, and the dip in this pool of potential college applicants is not expected to return to that level until at least 2023.

The declines vary by region, with substantial decreases in high-school graduates projected for states like Vermont, Ohio, and several others in the Northeast and Midwest, while states like Colorado, Nevada, Texas, and Utah and other states in the West and in the South are projected to see increases.

The shrinking pool of high-school graduates will also include more students from low-income households and lower-performing high schools. That means more of the students heading to college will require more in financial aid to be able to afford it—and increasing competition among colleges for the students who can afford to pay more. For community colleges and less-selective institutions, it will also mean more costs for remedial assistance.

Why have some public colleges emphasized recruiting of out-of-state and international students? Will this help their financial picture?

To bolster their bottom lines, some colleges have been relying on recruiting wealthy international students who can afford their tuition and, in the case of public colleges, out-of-state students who also pay higher rates than do the in-state students. At the University of Oregon, for example, the ratio of in-state to out-of-state went from 70:30 in 2003 to 55:45 in the span of a decade (although overall, the number of in-state students did not fall that much because the university expanded its enrollment to accommodate the out-of-staters).[50] Arizona State University, which already increased its proportion of out-of-state students from about 25 percent in the fall of 2002 to more than 31 percent, is looking especially to California to fill its pipeline, even going so far as to buy advertising space on the bins that travelers put their shoes in when going through security checks at several Southern California airports.

But experts are beginning to question the financial sustainability, political riskiness, and even the ethics of these strategies. While colleges contend that they recruit international and out-of-state students to increase diversity on their campuses, in states like Washington, lawmakers have responded by passing legislation requiring that the University of Washington accept at least four thousand state residents in each freshman class. The growing proportion of out-of-state students at flagship campuses has also raised political hackles in California, Virginia, and other states. Groups like the Western Interstate Commission on Higher Education have publicly questioned the impact of a recruiting strategy that allows colleges to effectively "swap similarly qualified students" with each other so they can reap the marginal additional revenue from the out-of-state rates they charge. "Good for the institutions but maybe not so good for the students," writes WICHE in a report that notes these students are paying more for "a substantially equivalent college experience."[51]

Meanwhile, colleges' pursuit of international students, who are sometimes charged additional fees on top of out-of-state tuition, has also prompted a bit of a backlash. In 2012, Chinese students at Purdue University waved banners protesting their being used as "cash cows" after the university said it would double to $2,000 the one-time fee it charges international students. More broadly, groups like WICHE have warned that the focus on full-pay international students could crowd out deserving domestic students, particularly those who are poor and members of minority groups.

Don't multimillion dollar broadcast contracts for football and basketball games and apparel-licensing deals produce big windfalls for colleges?

Such deals can produce revenue, but typically only for a few institutions. For the most part, even among the universities with big-time sports programs (mainly football and men's basketball), only a few break even. Data that is regularly compiled by *USA Today* and Indiana University's National Sports Journalism Center show that of the 228 public universities that operate Division I programs, only twenty-three took in more from tickets, licensing, broadcast deals, and donations than they spent on athletics in 2012. And even among those that generated surpluses, sixteen still received subsidies from other university funds. The nearly 350 public and private institutions in the National Collegiate Athletic Association's Division I are the colleges that maintain the largest athletic budgets, field teams in the most sports, and offer the most scholarships. (In Division II, with nearly three hundred colleges, institutions offer fewer athletics scholarships, while the 444 in Division III do not award any scholarships based purely on athletics.)

Given the focus on rising college costs, the role played by spending on college athletics has received relatively little public scrutiny until recently, perhaps because many taxpayers and students believe that the sports programs are more self-sufficient than they really are and, perhaps just as likely, because college sports are popular with alumni and political leaders. Now, however, the Knight Commission on Intercollegiate Athletics—an organization founded in 1989 to combat concerns about athletes' academic cheating scandals and growing commercialism—is trying to raise the visibility of the issue. Using data from *USA Today* and federal sources, the commission produced its own database that showed that athletics spending per athlete grew faster than academic spending per student from 2005 to 2011, particularly at colleges in Division I that participate in post-season football bowl games.[52] The disparity was smallest at colleges without football. The commission also found that costs for intercollegiate athletics are rising faster than other university expenses, and that "coaches' salaries and facility expenses are increasing at unsustainable rates."

Recent reporting by others supports those conclusions: *USA Today* found that seventy football coaches at public colleges were paid more than $1 million in 2013, and at private colleges, an analysis of salaries by *The Chronicle of Higher Education* found that thirty-three coaches and athletics directors topped $1 million in pay in 2011, the latest year for which that data were available. Data on facilities spending are hard to track because the NCAA and other organizations do not regularly collect it, and colleges often fold in their debt for stadiums and the like with bond issues for other campus facilities. But anecdotal reports have found that from 2000 until the 2008 financial crisis, institutions like Universities of Akron and Central Florida, and Oklahoma State and Rutgers Universities, bulked up on athletics facilities, some with borrowed money, raising concerns from rating agencies and others about their ability to repay the debt.[53]

The Knight Commission's data show that spending for facilities, related debt service, and equipment accounted for 15 to 20 percent of Division I athletics-department budgets at public colleges in 2010. It also shows that for all but the top football colleges in Division I, subsidies from the universities and student fees accounted for 40 to 70 percent of athletics budgets.[54]

Many colleges charge students an annual athletics fee ranging from about $150 to $600 to cover some of the costs of sports teams. But in many cases, particularly at colleges without big-time football and basketball, the actual amounts supporting athletics programs are substantially greater than those fees because the colleges also subsidize them using other revenues. Jeff Smith, a business professor at the University of South Carolina-Upstate, looked at the public institutions in twenty-eight athletics conferences in Division I and found big disparities between the subsidy levels at colleges in the richest conferences and those in the rest. In rich conferences like the Big Ten, average subsidies were the equivalent of $61 for every student; in the Southeast Conference they were $109, and in the Big Twelve, $136. But at colleges in low-revenue conferences, the subsidies, also calculated on a per-student basis, ran five to nine times that amount. In three of those conferences that do not have lucrative TV contracts—the Big South, Northeast, and Mid-Eastern Athletic Conferences— the colleges' average subsidy to the athletics program was in excess of $1,000 per student.[55] Smith also looked at institutions individually, and found at least nineteen public colleges where the per-student subsidy was greater than 20 percent of the tuition price in 2011.

Both Smith and Richard Vedder, the director of the Center on College Affordability and Productivity and an economics professor at Ohio University, have questioned the morality of such high subsidies, particularly at universities that enroll a high proportion of low-income students and where the proportion of students who borrow money to attend college is higher. Nonetheless, many colleges are upping their sports profile. Since 2010, one out of four colleges in Division I has shifted to another conference, often shedding nearby opponents for the national exposure (and money) that comes from the more-lucrative TV contracts of their new conferences. Many of those shifts, like the moves by the University of Pittsburgh and Syracuse University into a conference that also includes the University of Miami, will require the colleges to spend even more for travel costs to games for their teams that do not generate income. The colleges argue that the overall financial benefit outweighs the costs.

The outsize role that sports plays in American higher education, not to mention the wider American culture, creates a conundrum for college leaders who often find themselves decrying the emphasis on athletics at the expense of academics while also pushing for costly upgrades to their athletics programs and facilities. Indeed in 2013, the President of the University of Maryland system, William E. Kirwan, was co-chairman of the Knight Commission, even as he championed a controversial decision to move Maryland's flagship university at College Park from the athletic conference that it had helped to found more than a half-century ago to one that included bigger media markets and promises of a bigger financial payoff. Earlier Maryland said it would be cutting seven low-revenue sports including swimming because of athletics-department deficits. Other universities, including Temple in Philadelphia, have since announced similar cuts.

Does intercollegiate athletics pay off for colleges in other ways?

Both inside and outside of Division I, colleges often see athletics as a crucial student-recruiting tool. Some small colleges facing enrollment challenges, for example, have started or revived their football programs as a way of enrolling more men (the ninety-six players on a football team, plus male fans). By one count, between 2008 and 2015, fifty colleges will have started or revived their football teams, most of them non–Division I institutions such as Dordt College in Iowa, the College of Idaho, and George Fox and Pacific Universities, both in Oregon. In a tactic that is less-discussed publicly, some institutions eager to recruit wealthier full-pay students also sometimes add or upgrade the status of athletic programs like golf and lacrosse, which tend to be played in more upscale high schools.

Colleges also contend that successful sports teams can have a broader indirect financial benefit by building alumni and donor support. Yet some studies suggest that much of the money donated in the wake of winning seasons typically benefits athletics programs, not academic ones, and that any boon in giving is often short lived.[56]

Do universities make money on the drugs and other inventions that they patent and license?

A few institutions make a lot of money—hundreds of millions in the case of places like Columbia, New York, and Northwestern Universities, which in recent years have each shared in the riches from lucrative patents. (Columbia's patents paved the way for the creation of dozens of new drugs, NYU's for the anti-inflammatory drug Remicade, and Northwestern's for the anti-fibromyalgia drug Lyrica.) Most, however, do not.

This process of moving university inventions into the marketplace and into public use is known as "technology transfer." Some college leaders and outside consultants still see patenting and licensing as a promising source of income, and directors of technology transfer are sometimes hired and fired based on their records of generating income (much the way college basketball coaches are fired for losing seasons and admissions directors are let go for failing to "make their class.") But there is now also a school of thought that argues that generating revenues for the institution should not be the top priority for universities undertaking technology transfer; rather, they should see it as a service to their own faculty and as a means of promoting economic development. In 2010, a commission of the National Academy of Sciences even advised universities to be more realistic about their financial expectations.

By some estimates, most universities not only do not make much money from technology transfer, they actually lose money on it. One recent study that examined data from the 155 universities that reported patent and licensing data to the Association of University Technology Managers found that 130 of them did not generate enough in licensing income to cover the costs of their legal fees or salaries of their technology transfer officers in 2012. And that was a good year, the study found. On average over the past twenty years, 87 percent did not break even.[57]

What is the prognosis for revenue strategies that rely on "profits" from master's programs or law schools, or similar approaches based on internal cross-subsidies?

Most colleges operate on the basis of such cross subsidies, although these may be more complex at a big research university than at a small private liberal arts college. For many public and private colleges, master's degree programs—particularly those in education, business, and other fields that do not require expensive equipment—have operated as cash cows for institutions. Master's programs have also provided crucial financial support for a growing number of private liberal arts colleges, some of which tailor the programs for working adults with night and weekend schedules. Yet as we've seen, the competition for students in these programs has been heating up, with for-profit colleges taking bigger and bigger shares of this lucrative market. In 1996, more than half of all master's degrees were awarded by public colleges, but by 2012, that share had shrunk to 46 percent, while the for-profit sector, which held a negligible share in 1996, accounted for 10 percent. For-profit colleges have also gained ground in the growing market for certificates; they awarded 27 percent of all certificates in 2012, double their share in 1996, while the share awarded by public and private colleges had shrunk.

Law schools, too, were once significant sources of subsidy revenue, since by practice, the schools are "taxed" (as many law-school deans call it) as much as 30 percent of their tuition. But with law-school admissions plunging and many schools shrinking their own faculty ranks in the wake of the collapsing job market for lawyers, that revenue stream, too, is under strain.

Colleges also depend on other kinds of internal subsidies. The larger, introductory-level courses taken by freshmen and sophomores often cost less to offer than upper division and graduate courses, yet they are usually not priced any cheaper (although some institutions have begun to adopt tiered pricing). That means the students in these so-called lower-division courses are effectively subsidizing other classes that are more expensive to offer. Costs per upper division classes are about one-and-half-times more expensive to offer than lower division ones, according to one analysis. Leaving aside educational concerns of putting the least-experienced students into the largest classes (most of the student attrition comes in the first two years of college), and whether such pricing is fair to lower-division students, this financial strategy is now under threat from community colleges and alternative education providers offering their own versions of these "commodity courses" at a much lower cost than what colleges charges. One such alternative-education company, called StraighterLine, offers students hundreds of online courses for just $99-a-month for membership and $49 a course. It is just one example of many new ventures that aim to "unbundle" various aspects of the college experience, and with it, some of the revenue streams that undergird colleges' financial standing.

Are salaries of professors to blame for higher spending by colleges?

To be sure, professors are well paid compared to most Americans. In 2013–2014, average pay for an associate professor at public colleges was $80,448, and at private colleges it was $91,176. (Average salaries for public- and private-college full professors, the highest rank for tenured faculty members, were $112,897 and $144,770, respectively.)[58] The data come from the American Association of University Professors, an organization that produces an annual report offering the most comprehensive look at faculty pay. According to the AAUP, faculty pay is not the reason tuitions are rising. An analysis conducted by the association in 2012 showed that over the previous three decades, tuition rates have grown between three and fourteen times as fast as full-time faculty salaries, depending on the type of institution.[59]

The AAUP survey measures pay for faculty in two ways. One looks at the overall changes in pay levels for full-time professors. The other looks at how colleges' pay for their own professors' changes from year to year. In the decade ending 2014, average annual pay increases for full-time faculty overall did not exceed inflation in seven of the ten years. During the same period, however, colleges did provide raises to their own professors in excess of inflation every year except for two during the height of the financial crisis. In other words, salary increases for employed faculty were for the most part keeping up with inflation, but for people working as professors overall, pay was often not increasing as fast as inflation.[60]

One of the factors suppressing increases in average pay for full-time faculty is the growing reliance on full-time "contingent faculty"—that is, professors who work under annual or multi-year contracts, earning salaries that average about $45,000 a year. As of 2011 such professors made up 15 percent of the college-teaching workforce, up from 10 percent in 1975. During the same period, tenured professors and professors eligible for tenure became rarer and rarer. Less than a quarter of all college instructors in 2011 were tenured or on the tenure track, according to the AAUP's latest estimates. In 1975 about 45 percent were.[61]

The figures on average faculty pay reflect the salaries for full-time contingent faculty but do not take into account the much-lower salaries paid to part-time "adjunct" instructors. Adjuncts now make up 40 percent of all college instructors. (The remaining 20 percent of the faculty workforce is made up of graduate students who work as teaching assistants.) Adjuncts are paid per class they teach—and not much at that. A survey conducted by the Coalition on the Academic Workforce in 2010 that looked at more than ten thousand adjuncts teaching more than nineteen thousand courses found the average pay was about $2,700 a course.

As for the impact of faculty pay on college costs, studies by the Delta Cost Project show the proportion of college spending on "education and related" costs that went to faculty pay declined between 1998 and 2008 at every kind of institution studied, while costs for counseling, libraries, technology, and administration rose. "The common myth that spending on faculty is responsible for continuing cost escalation is not true," the report concluded.[62]

So what about the spending on these noninstructional costs? Is "administrative bloat" a factor in rising prices?

Few topics invite as much scorn for colleges as the subject of "administrative bloat." Over the past decade a number of studies and even some books have sought to document an undue increase in the number of nonacademic employees on colleges' payrolls as signs of inefficiency and misplaced spending priorities. While these studies often strike a chord by noting the proliferation of associate vice provosts and other bureaucratic sounding titles—or "deanlets" as author Benjamin Ginsberg calls them in his book *The Fall of the Faculty*—the findings often do not fully reflect the changes in how universities operate that have taken place during the same period. As this author herself observed in reporting about the University of Kansas, a major flagship university where the student body remained the same size from 1988 to 2008 but spending increased threefold, the expansion of student services, the increasing sophistication of sponsored research, and even the growing use of information technology has required additional hiring of nonacademic personnel.[63] Whether these changes require all the administrators and other staff that some of the colleges have hired in marketing, grants management, fundraising, public relations, real-estate management, and countless other operations— "enrollment communications strategist" was a job recently advertised by a Colorado public college—is an entirely different question. No doubt, most colleges have vastly bigger bureaucracies than a few decades ago. But it is also true that some reports on "bloat" clump together categories of managerial and professional employees as "administrators," who may in fact be working directly with students.

Except for one study by the State Higher Education Executives group defending hiring levels at public universities, most reports decry the administrative expansion. Ginsberg notes that in 1975, America's colleges employed more professors than administrators. Back then, he found, the work of 446,830 professors was supported by 268,952 administrators and staffers. Over the next four decades, the number of full-time professors or "full-time equivalents" increased slightly more than 50 percent, a rate that he says was comparable to the growth in student enrollments during the same time period. But the number of administrators increased by 95 percent and the number of administrative staffers by 240 percent.[64]

Another analysis focusing on a more-current period came in 2010 from Jay P. Greene and two associates through the Goldwater Institute. It analyzed data from 198 research universities and found that from 1993 to 2007 the number of full-time administrators per one hundred students increased by 39 percent, while the number of employees engaged in teaching, research, and public service—the three core missions of universities—grew by only 18 percent. Greene, a professor at the University of Arkansas, also looked at the costs of such personnel shifts and found that inflation-adjusted spending on administration increased by 61 percent compared to 39 percent for the spending on instruction. Greene's study argued that government subsidies facilitated the growth in administrative spending.[65]

More recently, a study by two other professors looked at the trend in a different way, comparing administrators to tenured professors and those on the tenure track. Examining data from 137 top public universities and sixty private institutions, Robert E. Martin of Centre College and R. Carter Hill of Louisiana State University found that between 1987 and 2011, the number of full-time nonacademic staff per professor doubled at public universities, and increased by 47 percent at private ones. They also found that universities substituted contract faculty and part-time faculty for tenure-track faculty during this period. Martin and Hill question how increasing the ratio nonacademic professional staff relative to tenure-track faculty is consistent with increasing the quantity and quality of teaching and research. "Tenure track faculty members are essential to both missions," the authors argue, "while nonacademic staff members are not."[66]

A Delta Cost Project analysis on higher education staffing trends over two decades showed substantial growth in administrative hiring across all sectors of higher education. It also found the biggest increases were for professional staff—business analysts, human-resources personnel, computer administrators, admissions officers, student counselors, and the like. (The study also found that colleges were becoming increasingly reliant on graduate assistants to handle teaching duties—so much so that public research universities now employ as many teaching assistants as they do full-time professors.) At community colleges and public colleges that offer master's and bachelor's degrees, the number of professional staff employees increased by about 150 percent from 1990 to 2012. By contrast, during the same period, the increase in the number of full-time faculty at public master's universities was just 18 percent, at public bachelor's 38 percent, and at community colleges, 31 percent.[67]

According to the latest available data from the Department of Education, the number of full-time "executive, administrative, and managerial" employees at all degree-granting colleges increased by more than 58 percent between fall 2001 and fall 2011, compared to an increase of 23 percent for the number of full-time faculty. The disparity was smaller when counting both full-time and part-time hires. But even then, the increase in that nonfaculty category far outpaced the rate of growth for faculty.

Overall, as of fall 2011, the 7,300-plus colleges and universities that take part in federal student-aid programs (those required to supply data to the U.S. Department of Education) employed more than 2.4 million people full time as professors, instructors, administrators, and technicians and another 1.4 million in a part-time capacity.[68]

Do those "lazy rivers" and other elements of the "amenities race" drive up college costs?

No doubt they do, although experts note that personnel, not buildings, account for 60 to 70 percent of spending by colleges. And according to an analysis by a company called Sightlines, about half of the buildings constructed during the twenty-five-year building boom that began on college campuses in the early 1990s were academic buildings, including many specially built to accommodate the needs of modern science. Another 25 percent of construction was directed at residential space, as colleges in some cases were knocking down or renovating older dormitories with gang showers in the bathrooms and replacing them with suites and apartment units that would be more appealing to a new generation of students.

That said, many of the academic fitness centers, student centers, and residence halls that accounted for the rest of the building boom seem plenty lavish: a residence hall at St. Leo University in Florida with a 2,100-gallon aquarium and nap pods; a fitness center at Boston University with a fifteen-person hot tub; a wellness center at the College of New Rochelle in New York featuring a meditation garden, to name just a few. Countless critics have heaped scorn on colleges for taking part in these so-called climbing-wall wars, even as many experts maintain that colleges, particularly those in rural locations, believed they would lose students to competing colleges if they did not buy into the race. Some economists have also questioned the morality of colleges bundling the costs for these amenities into their prices, which in effect requires students to borrow to pay for these luxuries.

Little research has been done to assess the impact of this spending spree, but one study that did found that prospective students actually do appreciate the added amenities (not only the facilities but the activities that come with them). But the study also found that for high-achieving high-school students, investments in academics mattered more, so if colleges were counting on the amenities to help them raise their academic profile, they might be disappointed.[69]

What about colleges' debt?

That too has raised some alarms. As the *New York Times* reported, the overall level of outstanding debt at the five hundred-plus public and private colleges and universities rated by Moody's more than doubled in inflation-adjusted dollars to $205 billion between 2002 and 2011, and colleges' payments for interest on that debt grew by more than 60 percent during the same period. Some of the money went for those amenities described above, now familiar landmarks of what has become known as the "edifice complex." A lot of it also went toward upgrading and constructing academic buildings, particularly for the sciences.

In fact, some of this borrowing was financially prudent, given the unusually low interest rates in the past few years, and some of the increase in interest payments was the result of colleges shifting from lower-cost but riskier variable rate debt to higher-cost but more conservative fixed-rate debt. Still, some analysts, including Bain Consulting and Sterling Partners, have criticized colleges for becoming "overleveraged." Bain and Sterling looked at nearly 1,700 private and public colleges and found that from 2002 to 2008, institutions had increased their long-term debt by nearly 12 percent and their interest expenses by more than 9 percent, while spending for instruction grew by just under 5 percent. Based in part on those rising debt levels, they suggested that as many as a third of colleges were on an unsustainable financial path, although that conclusion might have been skewed by comparisons of debt to endowment values which dropped steeply in 2008.[70] It should also be noted that Bain has its own self-interest in highlighting these trends; the consulting company is one of several firms wooing major universities to hire it to advise them on how to reduce spending.

However, some academics have also called the borrowing binge into question, with one from the Scholars Strategy Network calling it a piece of "a systematic problem" contributing to rising college costs, particularly at public colleges. After analyzing data from 155 public research universities and finding that their debt-service payments had risen 86 percent from 2002 to 2010, the scholars' network argued in a report that the universities were passing on that debt to students by raising tuition and fees by an average of 56 percent during the same period. As co-author Charlie Eaton maintained to Don Troop of *The Chronicle of Higher Education,* colleges with more amenities can get better credit ratings from agencies like Moody's because they can attract more higher-paying students from out of state. "But that may well be in conflict with this other priority that some folks have laid out of trying to keep college costs down both for students and taxpayers."[71]

Debt is also an issue for smaller colleges, many of which lack the financial wherewithal to obtain a rating from Moody's or Standard & Poor's. The Council of Independent Colleges maintains its own index of financial health for small and mid-sized private liberal arts colleges and universities. Debt levels are a key part of that index. From 2005 through 2011, the colleges with the smallest enrollments (fewer than 750 students) failed to meet even the minimum threshold of financial health. The financial health of all seven hundred institutions in the index suffered during the financial crisis, but while most quickly recovered enough to again pass the minimum threshold of that index, most of the smallest institutions did not.

What other things contribute to rising college costs?

Along with the higher spending for new dorms and buildings and the salary and benefit costs for the growth in administration, experts point to several other causes for the rise in college costs. Among them: "mission creep" and reductions of faculty teaching loads, and "buy downs" of faculty time for research.

In the status-conscious landscape of higher education, "mission creep" is a term often used when colleges try to become more like the institutions regarded as higher-up on the academic food chain—such as when a public college founded as an undergraduate institution adds master's programs or more research expectations for its faculty, for example. While these ambitions can certainly help diversify an institution and make it more attractive to students and professors, they also often drive up expenses and duplicate programs that may already exist nearby.

Smaller teaching loads can also add to costs. When senior professors are allowed lighter teaching loads, their departments must still offer enough courses to satisfy student needs and pay other professors or adjuncts extra to teach them. In cases where the professors are teaching a lighter load because they are spending more time on research, the costs are sometimes covered by funds from their research budgets. But that is not always the case. Many longtime higher education observers see teaching loads as a key variable in the college-cost equation, but it has been a difficult subject to study on a broad scale because national data on teaching-load trends have not been kept consistently.

Are there financial threats from other looming costs, like deferred maintenance?

For many colleges, the failing roofs, leaky windows, and balky boilers are financial ticking time bombs. The cost of deferred maintenance is enormous and the prospects for finding money to cover it are not. States, as previously discussed, are increasingly less able or inclined to come up with the billions needed. And donors, however generous, are far more likely to write a check to construct a new building rather than re-wire an older one.

There are no reliable figures on the cost of the maintenance backlog on American college campuses. Public estimates have ranged from $36 billion to more than $100 billion, but even those likely undercount the actual costs, judging by the figures individual campuses and university systems have reported in recent years: $400 million at the University of Maine system; $1.6 billion at the University of Massachusetts at Amherst;

$680 million at the Minnesota State Colleges and Universities; $500 million at Illinois State University; and $450 million at the University of New Mexico.[72]

The problem is compounded by the building profile at many campuses. As the consulting company Sightlines has documented, in the past sixty-five years, American colleges have undergone two major waves of campus construction. One came in the 1960s and 1970s, when the population of baby boomers was peaking on campuses; the second kicked off in the early 1990s, when factors like competition for students and the desire for more sophisticated and energy-efficient buildings drove construction demand. Some of the newer structures are notable for their energy-saving and environmentally friendly features. Colleges have built or overhauled more than three thousand buildings that are now registered or certified in the Leadership in Energy and Environmental Design program. But buildings have lifecycles, and as Sightlines and others have noted, those constructed in each of these eras are now coming due for their twenty-five- and fifty-year renewals. And while it is true that many of the newer buildings include features that require less spending on utilities and the like, it is also the case that the complex systems that undergird such structures also require more expertise and attention to keep them running well. Without that attention, and spending, the energy efficiency and waste removal systems of the buildings suffer.

Part Three

WHO'S IN CHARGE? LEADERSHIP PRESSURES— FROM WITHIN AND WITHOUT

How are colleges run? Is their unusual practice of "shared governance" in danger?

Public and private colleges are run by the governing boards that have fiduciary responsibility for them—be they the self-perpetuating boards of trustees that run private colleges, the politically appointed (and in some cases elected) boards of regents that oversee public colleges and public-college systems, or the elected trustees at many community colleges. But for nearly a century, colleges have also followed principles first articulated in 1920 by the American Association of University Professors (AAUP), which established the idea that faculty and administrators share responsibility for running their colleges. In the mid-1960s, these principles were actually codified in a document signed onto by the AAUP, the Association of Governing Boards, and the American Council on Education, the umbrella association of college presidents.

Most colleges also ostensibly adhere to ideals set out in a 1940 AAUP statement of principles that states: "Institutions of higher education are conducted for the common good and not to further the interest of either individual teacher or the institution as a whole. The common good depends upon the free speech for truth and its exposition. Academic freedom is essential to these purposes."

There has never been a firm definition of what policies are covered by "shared governance," but generally it is the reason college decision making about new buildings, new majors, changes to teaching loads, the selection of a new president, and in some cases, new research relationships, traditionally has involved committees, input by faculty senates, and other forms of consultation that are not found in typical corporate hierarchies.

Today, as some institutions have become more sophisticated in their operations (running extensive online undertakings and big-time athletics programs) and more businesslike in their management style, faculty groups on some campuses worry that decisions that once fell under the purview of "shared governance," such as decisions about offering new online degrees, are now being handled by administrators, or that the consultation is more *pro forma* than genuine. The effectiveness of shared governance has also been weakened by universities' shift away from hiring tenured and tenure-track faculty, although in some cases, it is the faculty groups themselves that bar part-timers from full-fledged membership in the academic senates and governance bodies that represent faculty members' interests. In other instances, most notably at some California community colleges, policy advocates have argued that faculty senates have used the guise of "shared governance" to block even the most modest of changes to curricula and advising procedures.

The weakening of shared governance is hard to quantify, but in a poll conducted in May 2013 by Gallup and the online publication *Inside Higher Ed*, nearly one of five college presidents agreed that shared governance was "no longer respected by their governing boards as it was in the past."[1] Some observers say the waning of faculty power is less prevalent at major research universities that depend on the revenue that their professors bring in from research grants, and more so at the larger majority of institutions that are more dependent on tuition and state funds and where professors have less financial clout.

At the same time, accreditors, credit-rating agencies, advocacy groups, and college presidents themselves have been voicing doubts about the effectiveness of college governance writ large, particularly as higher education faces continued financial challenges, public doubts about its value, and political pressure from the White House on down. A top executive at Moody's Investors Service, for example, has said a common element his agency finds at institutions in financial distress is often "a terrible board, or worse, a terrible president."[2] The agency has also said it could lower credit ratings of poorly run institutions. In another Gallup-*Inside Higher Ed* survey, only 45 percent of four-year, private college presidents strongly agreed they were confident their institution was well-governed by its board; of presidents at four-year public colleges, only one of five did.[3]

Some observers say the problems with higher-education governance are also reflected in the seeming rise in the number of campuses where faculty have approved votes of "no confidence" in their institution's leadership and in high-profile political battles between presidents and factions of their governing boards, like those at the University of Texas at Austin in 2013 and University of Virginia in 2012. Also, while hardly a typical higher-education issue, the revelations in 2012 of child sex-abuse charges against one of Pennsylvania State University's former assistant football coaches, followed by criticism and legal action that questioned the president's and board of trustees' handling of those charges, also revealed failures in the way they and other colleges' leaders oversee their institutions.

Organizations like the American Council of Trustees and Alumni, meanwhile, contend that many trustees are not doing enough to rein in spending at their own colleges for things like underperforming academic programs and capital spending. The organization annually publishes the "What Will They Learn" report that critiques colleges with poor graduation rates that fail to offer a more traditionalist curriculum and an environment for "unfettered free speech."

Governance is an entirely different matter at for-profit colleges, where corporate-style decision-making has always been the norm. As discussed previously in Part Two, for-profit colleges include small family-owned enterprises, small and not-so-small chains owned by private investor groups and private-equity funds, and giant publicly traded corporations like Apollo and DeVry. At these companies, the corporate board of directors has final say, although in some cases, accreditors have required colleges to establish boards of trustees to oversee academic matters.

What role do adjunct professors play in this system?

Initially, adjunct instructors were prevalent only at community colleges. Often they were working professionals, hired with the idea that they could bring their real-world expertise into the classroom. Over time, four-year colleges began to employ them, too. They supplemented the teaching ranks that were otherwise filled by full-time professors who had earned doctorates and similar credentials, and then entered higher education as instructors or assistant professors, hoping to eventually earn full professorships and tenure. Those working-professional adjuncts still exist. But many colleges have also turned many of the traditionally trained PhD holders and other aspiring professors into adjuncts. Many in the public think of colleges as institutions filled with professors who enjoy guaranteed lifetime employment. In fact, as we saw in the previous chapter, adjuncts, including those hired to handle a class or two plus others on full-time annual contracts (also called "contingent faculty"), now collectively make up about 60 to 70 percent of the professoriate.

The part-time adjuncts generally have no role in campus governance. The estimated 285,000 or so adjuncts who work full-time under one-year or multiyear contracts but are not "on the tenure track" have a little more say in academic matters, although some are still excluded from even their own department's decision-making on curriculum and other matters.

For the most part, adjuncts, whose jobs depend on the shifting needs of colleges, resent their limited influence and low status in the academic hierarchy. As described by the New Faculty Majority, a leading organization for adjunct rights founded in 2009, "college instructors have seen their profession turn into low-wage, part-time, unbenefited jobs rather than into respected employment capable of supporting a family." The New Faculty Majority and other adjunct groups also say that the poor working conditions and prevalence of adjuncts hurts students' opportunities for academic success because the part-timers are not given the resources or time to properly advise their students.[4] A few studies have echoed those concerns although the issue has not been widely researched.

Through such organizations as the New Faculty Majority and others like Adjunct Nation, the Coalition on the Academic Workforce, and the Delphi Project on the Changing Faculty and Student Success and through unions like the American Federation of Teachers, the Service Employees International Union, and even the United Steelworkers, adjuncts have been organizing for official recognition, higher pay, health-care benefits, and better working conditions, such as office space. On some campuses, adjunct-faculty unionizing campaigns have been met with strong opposition from college leaders, some of whom have even hired law firms known for their union-opposition work in the corporate world. In 2013, adjuncts at several Catholic and Lutheran colleges took an even more unusual organizing tack, publicly invoking religious teachings about workers' rights to organize. That cause gained ground after the story of Mary Vojtko became a public rallying cry for adjuncts. Vojtko was an eighty-three-year-old adjunct instructor at Duquesne University who died nearly penniless and without health insurance after teaching at the Pittsburgh institution for twenty-five years.

The adjunct cause has also been taken up by some scholarly societies, agencies that accredit colleges, and a faculty group called the Campaign for the Future of Higher Education, which seeks greater public investment in higher education and opposes what it calls "simplistic" metrics for evaluating colleges and "false economies" made in the name of efficiency. Another venture known as The Adjunct Project, created in 2012 by a part-time English composition instructor at the University of Georgia named Josh Boldt, provides adjuncts a crowd-sourced tool with information on adjunct pay at thousands of colleges so they can compare pay levels and see if what they are being offered is fair. (The Adjunct Project is now part of *The Chronicle of Higher Education*.) The issue has also caught the attention of some in Congress. In 2014, Democrats on a House of Representatives education committee issued a report warning that the rise of "piece work" pay in higher education posed a threat to the quality of higher education and to the profession of college teaching.[5]

How do the faculty models at large for-profit colleges compare with those of traditional institutions? Are these "core faculty" models catching on in traditional higher education?

Unlike most traditional colleges, for-profit colleges do not offer tenure, pledge fealty to the principles of academic freedom, or expect that their teaching faculty members will also conduct original research or undertake public service. Moreover, at the vast majority of large for-profit colleges, most faculty members do not play a role in developing the courses that they teach. Instead, the colleges follow what might be called a more industrialized model. Typically, the colleges rely on a small group of faculty and deans who decide the content of courses and majors. The colleges then hire hundreds (or in the case of giant for-profit institutions like the University of Phoenix and Kaplan University, thousands) of adjunct instructors to teach these standardized courses. Phoenix, for example, employs about 29,000 faculty members, most of them part-timers, who teach its 250,000 students, but fewer than one thousand faculty members have any real say over what is taught.

This "industrial" model can be profitable: As one adjunct instructor wrote to the congressional committee looking at the changing academic labor market: "Considering that students pay $565 per course, and that there are approximately twenty students per class, adjuncts are paid approximately 4% of what the university takes in even though we execute the core requirements of the university."[6]

In the past few years, a small but growing number of entrepreneurial nonprofit colleges, particularly those with large distance-education programs and substantial continuing education operations, have adopted some version of this model where the traditional holistic responsibilities of professors—to decide what goes into a class, create it, teach it, advise students, and give out grades—are "unbundled" into separate duties and parceled out in part to nonfaculty or outsourced to private companies. It is the model, for example, at Southern New Hampshire University's fast-growing College of Online and Continuing Education and at National University based in San Diego. The nonprofit, 40,000-student Western Governors University, a fully online university created by state governors in the mid-1990s, disaggregates the faculty role in a different way. It uses "program faculty" to help develop its curriculum, other faculty with subject-matter knowledge as "course mentors" to oversee the self-paced instruction, and yet another group of faculty known as "evaluators" to grade students' work. Indeed, as one scholar looking at online courses in general has noted, the "unbundling" of a faculty member's role in teaching a course can now be divided into nine discrete functions, including instructional design, tutoring, course delivery, and, advising.[7] Many of these functions can be handled by someone other than the professor, and at some institutions, increasingly they are.

College leaders say models like this allow them to more efficiently "scale" up their programs and meet the demands of more students while also guaranteeing that courses satisfy quality standards set by the institution or a department. But many faculty members believe such approaches devalue the role of individual professors and deprive students of meaningful interactions with instructors steeped in the knowledge of their disciplines. Some also worry that the model fundamentally weakens the role of the professoriate itself, by shifting control over the curriculum away from those who teach and who have historically had final say over such matters.

What concerns have been raised about the future of the college presidency?

College presidents as a group are graying—well over half of them were sixty-one years or older in 2011, compared with just 14 percent in 1986, the first year the American Council on Education began surveying them. The share of presidents aged fifty or younger declined from 42 percent to 10 percent in the same period. With a wave of retirements expected in the next few years, and the tenure of typical presidencies growing shorter (the average is now seven years, down from eight-and-a-half in 2006), some observers worry that higher education will soon be facing a leadership vacuum just as the challenges of running a college are growing increasingly complex. At the same time, some note that this turnover could also present opportunities for increasing diversity in the presidential ranks, so that higher-education leaders will be more reflective of the institutions they head. In 2011, only about a quarter of all college presidents were women and only 13 percent were members of a racial or an ethnic minority group. (That latter figure was even lower—just 9 percent—if you exclude those at historically black and other minority-serving institutions).[8]

At the nation's 1,200 two-year public colleges, the turnover has already begun. Between 2012 and 2013, some two hundred new presidents took the helm at community colleges. By 2018, another five hundred presidents are expected to have retired, many of them long-serving executives who led their institutions during the sector's four decades of expansion, according to an analysis by the American Association of Community Colleges.[9] Now, with community colleges facing particular pressures to preserve their open-access mission in the face of diminished public funding, groups like the Aspen Institute say the colleges face "a moment of crisis and opportunity" as they select their next generation of presidents.[10]

Also, while public colleges are always subject to political forces, such tensions have been particularly acute for presidents of public research universities, which have become a frequent target of criticism for Republican governors in states like Florida, North Carolina, Texas, and Wisconsin. Public research institutions sit at the crucible of many of the political and economic challenges facing colleges today, and their leaders are less insulated from public pressures than those who run private colleges. The Association of American Universities represents leading research universities, of which thirty-four are public institutions based in the United States. From mid-2011 to early 2014, sixteen presidents of that thirty-four quit or were fired—and that does not count University of Virginia President Teresa A. Sullivan, who was fired by her board in 2012 and then reinstated two weeks later.

Do American colleges face international competition?

The United States is still the number one destination for undergraduate and graduate students who leave their home country to study abroad. In 2012–2013, according to the latest annual "Open Doors" report, a record number of international students—nearly 820,000—enrolled in American colleges. China sends the most, about 29 percent of the total, followed by India,

South Korea, Saudi Arabia, and Canada. International students make up 3.9 percent of overall college enrollment in the United States. But according to figures released in 2013 by the Organization for Economic Cooperation and Development, America's share of the international student market fell between 2000 and 2010, while Australia's and the United Kingdom's rose.

Foreign students are not the only ones interested in American-style education. So too are some foreign governments and philanthropies. On the outskirts of Doha, the capital of Qatar, sits a still-developing $3 billion Education City. Begun in the late 1990s with financing from a Qatari foundation, Education City is now home to eight overseas institutions, six of which are American: Carnegie Mellon, Georgetown, Northwestern, Texas A&M, and Virginia Commonwealth Universities, and the Weill Cornell Medical College. Separately, in 2010, with financing from the government of Abu Dhabi, the new liberal-arts campus of New York University began enrolling its first students in what will eventually be a campus for about two thousand. These ventures, along with a new Yale University venture with the National University of Singapore and Duke University's planned business school in Kunshan, China, are relatively small. In some quarters, they are also controversial with faculty and others who say the institutions legitimize societies that do not fully respect human rights or fully embrace academic freedom. But they are one more sign of the high regard in which American universities—at least top ones—are held in other countries.

To the point of cliché, college leaders often proclaim American higher education as the "envy of the world." And by all measures, institutions in the United States continue to rank highly among the three major international ratings. American institutions account for all but two of the top ten institutions in the Shanghai Jiao Tong University's rankings out of China; they make up eleven of the twenty highest-ranked by a British company known as QS; and on the *Times Higher Education*'s

2013 World University Rankings, forty-five of the top one hundred colleges are from the United States. The international rankings rate only research institutions.

But as Karin Fischer reported in *The Chronicle of Higher Education* in 2013, beyond the very top institutions, America has slipped some. There are thirty fewer American universities on the latest Shanghai ranking than there were when it was first published a decade ago; on the others, the majority of American institutions have slipped below previous rankings. And, she notes, a 2010 study by Australian researchers found that, given its size and financial resources, the United States actually underperforms in the rankings: It should have about 10 percent more universities on the Shanghai list than it does, they concluded.

What do people mean when they talk about the "accountability movement" in higher education?

The phrase "accountability movement" is generally applied to the growing interest from political leaders, taxpayers, and outside advocates who are asking colleges to demonstrate in measurable ways that they are making good use of tuition dollars and public funds. Typically, that has translated into greater attention from lawmakers, policy advocates, and parents about student outcomes like graduation rates, whether students are amassing excess credits before they graduate, and what kind of job and salary they land after they graduate. One new organization that owes its existence to this movement is called College Measures, which has tapped into state employment data, and is now working in several states to provide policy makers with comparative information on the salaries of graduates from various academic programs.

A key piece of the accountability movement is known as "the completion agenda," a broad-based push by student advocates, policy makers, and education-focused associations and foundations to improve colleges' graduation rates and also collect more and better data about how students are progressing toward their degrees. In some cases, the demands for accountability lead to pressure on institutions to explain things like their cost per graduate, the workload of faculty members, and professors' research output. One short-lived effort at the Texas A&M system in 2010 even tracked and published data on the Internet on each professor's "bottom line," showing whether they made or lost money for the university based on their salaries, number of students taught, and value of their research grants.

Is the accountability movement having an impact?

The accountability movement now underlies many state policies toward colleges. At least twenty states have implemented "performance-based" funding, which ties state appropriations to public colleges to the accomplishment of certain goals, such as an increased graduation rate, lower student debt, or more students majoring in science, technology, engineering, and mathematics. Louisiana is looking into awarding some state funding based on how well colleges collaborate with local industries to produce graduates with "job-ready" degrees. Traditionally, colleges were funded primarily on their enrollments, not on outcomes like this. While in most of these states, the funding tied to performance still accounts for just a small piece of the overall spending on public colleges, in Ohio, funds tied to performance are slated to account for 30 percent of public colleges' appropriations by 2015, and in Tennessee, nearly all of the funding to higher education (some $1.5 billion in recent years) is awarded in this manner.

Some higher-education leaders complain that these accountability demands are often too simplistic and one-dimensional, and they note that focusing too heavily on one measure could come at the expense of another, particularly when a poor outcome could result in a cut in funding. A focus on improving graduation rates with a faster "time-to-degree," for example, could lead to higher completion rates but might not necessarily guarantee that students will have mastered a rigorous curriculum, a concern that has been raised by groups like the American Association of Colleges & Universities, which promotes educational practices that encourage such mastery and greater attention to academic rigor. Others note that such accountability demands could discourage colleges from admitting students who seem less likely to graduate. In 2013, two researchers at the University of Wisconsin, who studied smaller state experiments with performance-based funding from the 1990s and 2000s, concluded that "more often than not, performance funding failed to increase degree completions."[11] Some longtime higher-education observers also contend that states' interest in performance-based funding is a way to justify cuts to higher education.

In response to the public pressures, several higher-education groups have also created their own set of measures. Their names give a good picture of their intent, if not necessarily their effect: There is the "Voluntary Framework of Accountability" from the American Association of Community Colleges; the "Voluntary System of Accountability," from the Association of Public and Land-Grant Universities; and the "College Accountability Network," from the National Association of Independent Colleges and Universities. While the community-colleges framework aims to measure the broader activities that two-year colleges offer, such as the numbers of certificates they award, the other measures provide much of the same information that is already available in consumer guidebooks or on the Department of Education's "College Navigator" site.

Additionally, in 2013 the "Big Six" higher education organizations (the three mentioned above plus the American Association of State Colleges and Universities, the Association of American Universities, and the American Council on Education) established the "Student Achievement Measure." It offers comparisons of colleges' graduation rates in a manner that is more complete than official Department of Education data, which only counts first-time, full-time students and does not take into account the estimated 20 percent of students who transfer and later graduate from an institution other than the one where they started.

Some states and systems have created their own report cards as well, including "Compare College TX," in Texas, "The SUNY Report Card," produced by the State University of New York, and the "Student Success Scorecard" for the 112 institutions in the California Community College system. The degree to which students actually rely on such report cards in selecting a college is hard to know, but several education-policy experts say they could become valuable if college themselves use the data they contain on things like student retention as tools for regular self-improvement.

Do the reports and measures actually say much about what students learn?

In a sense, many of these measures are a proxy—some say an inadequate one—for what is harder to assess about college: the quality of its education and whether its students are learning. Colleges have historically resisted the notion that standard-ized tests and similar kinds of assessments could capture the essence of a college education, even though in the 1990s, there was an "assessment movement" in higher education that sought to develop more sophisticated measurements and pro-mote the practice. But the movement never really took hold and the association behind it folded in 2005, leaving authors who have studied the issue to argue that any presumptions about the quality of college's undergraduate education can only be "faith-based" at best because of the paucity of infor-mation. "Answers based on evidence are scarce," say Richard P. Keeling and Richard H. Hersh in their book, *We're Losing Our Minds*, "and few institutions of higher education have consented to having whatever data they have about student learning compared in any public way with data from other institutions—especially their competitors."[12] The critique echoed the indictment lodged in 2006 by a commission headed by then-Secretary of Education Margaret Spellings, which faulted higher education for its "remarkable absence of accountability mechanisms to ensure that colleges succeed in educating students."[13]

Such external pressures may be having an effect; in 2014 a survey by the National Institute for Learning Outcomes Assessment found that increasing numbers of colleges were becoming more systematic in evaluating what students were learning, often at the request of their accreditors—although less than a third of the 1,200 institutions surveyed said they shared the results outside their own campuses.[14] A new effort spearheaded by higher-education officials in Massachusetts and the American Association of Colleges & Universities may help to shift that tide. Along with eight other states— Connecticut, Indiana, Kentucky, Missouri, Minnesota, Oregon, Rhode Island, and Utah—Massachusetts will be developing tests and tools to measure and compare what their students learn in college.

Is the federal government also looking to hold colleges accountable?

Without question, the federal government is focusing attention on college accountability, and the scope of that attention is expanding. Until recently, aside from policies aimed at colleges with high rates of default on student loans and other student-aid regulations, most of the federal emphasis on accountability has been centered on the price of college. In the Higher Education Act of 2008, for example, Congress mandated that the Department of Education annually post the prices of the most and least expensive colleges, and also show the 5 percent of colleges with the highest and lowest percentage increases in tuition and net price. Some experts fault this report, often referred to as the "shame lists," because the lack of context can bring unwarranted criticism to institutions that are still relatively inexpensive but just happened to have raised their tuition in a given year. A *Chronicle of Higher Education* analysis of colleges that have appeared repeatedly on the lists also found that it had little effect on colleges' prices.[15]

Beginning in 2012, President Obama also began campaigning against college costs. And in his 2013 State of the Union Address, Obama announced a new "College Scorecard," which he described as a tool to help students and their families see "where you can get the most bang for your educational buck." The College Scorecard is an interactive web site that provides information on colleges' graduation rates, costs, and average student-loan debt. It may eventually also include information on graduates' earnings. While some saw the move as step toward greater transparency on colleges' effectiveness, the Scorecard has been criticized for its reliance on incomplete data (it uses the federal official graduation rate) and on measures that might not be readily understandable to consumers, such as net price.

Later in 2013, President Obama and the Department of Education also announced plans to create a federal college ratings system that would evaluate colleges on a much broader set of measures, potentially including the proportion of financially needy students enrolled, affordability, rates at which community-college students transfer to four-year colleges, alumni satisfaction, and, most controversially, graduates' earnings. While this system, like the Scorecard, would be helpful to future students and their families, the Administration has also said it would like to tie levels of federal aid to the ratings by 2018—for example, offering higher Pell Grants and more-affordable student loans to higher-rated institutions—although such a major shift in policy would require Congressional approval.

Not surprisingly, the idea of creating such a high-stakes rating system drew objections from many higher-education leaders and observers. Some did welcome the idea, because it would create a visible alternative to the consumer rankings like *U.S. News & World Report*, which reward colleges more for inputs like high selectivity (and indirectly, spending), with one that would measure outputs such as access for low-income students and affordability. Most of the criticism, however, centered on whether the Education Department had valid data to make such evaluations given that the information in the federal Integrated Postsecondary Education Database System, the basis for most department reports, does not even measure all students who eventually graduate. Others have worried that a rating system that evaluates colleges based in part on the salaries of graduates would penalize institutions that prepare students in fields that are important to society but are lower-paying, such as teaching and social work. Many of these critics also questioned whether it is even appropriate to use financial measures like salaries to assess the value of a college education. And as with the state accountability movement, some said the rating system could have unintended consequences. Despite those criticisms, and some objections from members of Congress who see it as a government overreach, the Obama Administration has been pressing ahead with plans for the rating system.

Might these "accountability" pressures make their way into federal law?

Predicting what Congress will do is nearly impossible, of course, but it's very likely that lawmakers will embrace some version of these measures. Every five years or so Congress undertakes a major review of the Higher Education Act, the law that was first enacted in 1965 as part of Lyndon B. Johnson's Great Society agenda of domestic programs and now lays out rules for student aid. The act has been renewed (or in congressional parlance, reauthorized) nine times since then, most recently in 2008. Work on the latest reauthorization began in 2013, with most observers expecting that the final legislation will include new provisions that somehow use federal aid to reward and punish colleges on outcomes like graduation rates and affordability. It may also make changes in how accreditors evaluate colleges.

Why is there interest in changing what accreditors do?

Accreditors are hugely powerful gatekeepers, and lately many within and outside higher education have begun to question the entire process of accreditation. The system has many critics: colleges who say its arcane procedures are too cumbersome and too costly; policy advocates who say the system is too accepting of poor college performance; student advocates who say its actions are too opaque to provide strong consumer protection; and self-proclaimed education reformers who say it's too slow to recognize innovative approaches. Additionally, because the entire accreditation system is based on colleges being reviewed by colleagues from their peer institutions, the system is also sometimes attacked for being more club than watchdog.

Accreditation is nominally a "voluntary" way for colleges to provide assurances to students and others in the public that their offerings meet quality standards. But in reality it is essential, because degrees and credits from unaccredited institutions are often not taken seriously by employers, licensing agencies, or other colleges, and because in the United States, federal and state student aid is only provided to students at institutions approved by recognized accreditation bodies. As a consequence, while government has delegated some authority to accreditors to oversee colleges, it still has an interest (financial and otherwise) in assuring that the oversight is adequate.

Institutional accreditation is carried out by one of nineteen private organizations made up of member colleges.

(Another sixty or so organizations accredit individual programs in fields like business, engineering, and nursing.) Six of these organizations are "regional" accreditors whose members include most nonprofit and degree-granting institutions, plus a few for-profit colleges. The other accrediting bodies, known as "national" accreditors, have member institutions that include many more for-profit, non–degree-granting institutions, as well as religious seminaries. While each accrediting agency operates by its own standards and practices, each generally carries out accreditation by requiring institutions to conduct a self-study and undergo a periodic review and a site visit by a team of officials from other member colleges. Colleges can lose accreditation if they fail to satisfy the agencies' standards on such matters as financial viability, governance, or in the case of some national accreditors overseeing career-focused colleges, adequate job-placement for graduates—but few colleges ever do. More often they are placed on probation or given some other intermediate sanction and given time to improve.

As dissatisfaction with accreditation has grown, some in Washington, including the Obama Administration as well as others from outside government, have suggested creating an alternative to the existing accreditation system. The specifics of such proposals remain to be seen.

What other kinds of organizations are calling for a new direction in higher education? Is this kind of attention new?

You can tell American higher education is in the hot seat by the number of groups, pundits, and companies proposing ways to reform it, seemingly on a daily basis. This is a fairly new phenomenon. It's not that criticism from outside is new; the debates about speech codes and "political correctness" in the 1980s and the "Culture Wars" over the makeup of canon in fields like history and literature in the 1990s are just two recent examples of past external criticism. But until the early

2000s, most of the recommendations about how higher education functioned as an enterprise or industry came from within its own membership associations (there's an association for just about any slice of academe that one can imagine) or from established groups like the National Governors' Association and the Education Commission of the States.

Now, however, the list of organizations conducting research and issuing reports and polls on higher education has ballooned, encompassing groups across the political spectrum. In recent years, groups as diverse as the New America Foundation, the Center for American Progress, Public Agenda, the Brookings Institution, the American Enterprise Institute, the Urban Institute, and the U.S. Chamber of Commerce have all established programs specifically devoted to studying higher education, and they weigh in regularly with reports and research on things like ways to improve student-aid programs, graduate more students at less cost, and encourage more alliances with outside companies.

Some of the enterprises publicly weighing in also have a direct financial incentive. For example, as discussed in the previous chapter, Bain Consulting produced a report questioning the financial viability of hundreds of colleges even as it continues to seek major contracts with universities to hire it to advise them on how to operate more efficiently. McKinsey and Company, another consulting firm better known for its work in corporate settings but now vying for university clients, has also weighed in with reports proposing broad scale changes in higher education productivity. On the whole, the public attention these organizations are paying to topics like college productivity has raised their visibility and urgency to policymakers.

What role are big foundations playing in shaping the national higher-education agenda?

Foundations have always had an interest in higher education, but until recently, they tended to express it through grants to institutions or consortia to help develop new curricula, new ways of teaching, or new avenues of collaboration. It was through grants in the late 1960s from the Ford Foundation, for example, that colleges created Commonfund, a non-profit organization that now manages billions in endowment investments for thousands of colleges. The Carnegie Corporation and the Carnegie Foundation for the Advancement of Teaching, and the Ford, William and Flora Hewlett, Kresge, Andrew W. Mellon, Spencer, and Teagle Foundations all also continue to play influential roles. The Hewlett Foundation, for example, was a major backer of the Open Learning Initiative at Carnegie Mellon University, which is creating engaging online courses that allow for personalized teaching at a distance. The Carnegie Foundation is a key mover behind new approaches to teaching remedial mathematics called "Quantway" and "Statway." And the Mellon Foundation still funds efforts to promote research and teaching in the humanities.

But on the policy front, these foundations with traditional ties to higher education have been overshadowed in recent years both in spending and activity by two big and relatively newer players: the Bill & Melinda Gates Foundation and the Lumina Foundation for Education. According to an analysis by *The Chronicle of Higher Education*, between 2008 and 2013, the two foundations have pumped nearly $600 million into programs and organizations seeking to overhaul how higher education is financed, regulated, and delivered.[16] The Carnegie Corporation, Ford Foundation, Hewlett Foundation, and Kresge Foundation have also adopted this emphasis on "broad-scale higher-education issues such as completion, productivity, and technology" since 2000, according to researchers at the Claremont Graduate University.[17] But none of them have had as big an impact as Gates, the world's largest private grant-making foundation, or Lumina, the largest foundation devoted solely to higher education.

Gates and Lumina are key supporters of dozens of think tanks and advocacy groups pressing for reform, including controversial changes in remedial education, like those advocated by their grantee Complete College America (Gates actually helped create that organization), and for more leeway to allow federal student aid for self-paced degree programs, like those advocated by another grantee, the New America Foundation. Gates is also financing the AAC&U and Massachusetts effort to measure student learning. Both foundations say the changes are needed to create more opportunities for low-income and "first-generation" students to enter and graduate from a worthy college (or, in the case of Lumina, earn a worthwhile postsecondary credential short of a degree). Through a project called Reimagining Aid Design and Delivery, the Gates foundation has funded dozens of academic researchers to study how federal financial aid could be re-conceived to encourage faster student completion—a goal that some college leaders argue is "elitist" for failing to acknowledge the real financial pressures that sometimes drive needy students to take longer to graduate. And through an intermediary, the Gates foundation has also provided millions to start-up enterprises—some of them for-profit—that are building ventures like new low-cost online colleges. The grants are an effort to seed the education marketplace with new entrepreneurial models and build acceptance for ideas that might come from the private sector.

Bill Gates, the founder of Microsoft whose billions created his namesake foundation, has himself argued for more public policies that tie government support to higher college completion rates. "We cannot be agnostic about whether aid subsidizes failure or success," he said in a June 2012 speech to the Association of Public and Lang-Grant Universities.[18]

While few have taken issue with the broad goals of Gates and Lumina, some have questioned whether they are using their vast philanthropic resources to create a political consensus for their own preconceived ideas. Foundation officials rarely interact directly with legislators or members of

Congress, but their grantees often do. Along with dozens of other organizations, Gates and Lumina each also fund influential organizations like the research center at Teachers' College of Columbia University; the National Student Clearinghouse, which tracks students' progress through college; the Institute for Higher Education policy, which advocates for first-generation students; and Achieving the Dream, which studies educational practices at community colleges. With Gates and, to a lesser degree, Lumina putting money behind so many higher-education groups and studies, some professors and higher-education observers have grown wary of their growing influence. Foundation officials, however, say their philanthropy is helping to raise visibility for new ideas that push the higher-education enterprise toward needed changes.

Have nonprofit universities been "corporatized"?

Most observers would say yes, but there is hardly a common understanding of what the corporatization of college means. For some, it's the corporate-style salaries; at least forty-two private college presidents—not all of them heads of complex operations—earn more than a $1 million a year and dozens of other college employees (coaches and athletics directors, investment officers, and other administrators) now do, too.[19] For others it's the growth of the administrative bureaucracy and spending on areas like marketing and public relations, with the hiring of "vice-chancellors for marketing," branding consultants that specialize in higher education, and even firms that do polling now increasingly more commonplace practices. Still others cite the "adjunctification" of the faculty—a version of the outsourcing taking place in the broader economy.

Some critics also see the tuition models of colleges, in some cases brought on by states' disinvestment, as an indication of corporatized higher education, especially when it means students are left on the hook to pay loans off while banks still profit handsomely from the fees they get for servicing the loans and, in the case of private loans, from the interest borrowers pay. Since 2010, banks no longer play a role in originating federal student loans but some older federal loans, along with private ones, are still packaged and sold off as investments, much the way mortgages are "securitized." Companies like Sallie Mae still reap hundreds of millions in loan-servicing and delinquency-collection fees on student loans, too. In a 2014 report on Sallie Mae, the National Consumer Law Center called it a "student-debt fueled profit machine."[20]

Additional practices might also fall under the category of corporatization. Dozens of research universities now work hand-in-hand with companies on research into new drugs or fuels and offer those companies first crack at commercializing what they invent. Banks and other financial companies sign deals with colleges to offer debit and credit cards to students. Companies now also increasingly endow professorships that bear their names and provide donations that allow them naming rights on buildings. (One such proposal in 2013 would have named the new stadium at Florida Atlantic University for a local and controversial private-prison company, until the company withdrew its $6 million offer amid student and faculty protests.)

The millions that some colleges earn from TV and licensing deals, meanwhile, has prompted a former University of California at Los Angeles basketball player named Ed O'Bannon to pursue a class-action lawsuit demanding that college athletes receive a share of the revenue that colleges earn from broadcasts, merchandise, and even video games that use likenesses of players. There is even a fledgling effort, spurred by athletes at Northwestern University, to allow students on athletics scholarships to unionize and bargain for better concussion prevention and other athlete needs. When that unionizing effort received its initial okay from the National Labor Relations Board in spring 2014, based on evidence that athletes were being asked to spend far more hours in training and practices than in their studies, commentators and others called it yet one more sign that commercial forces were overtaking higher-education values at colleges with big-time athletics programs.

On a more subtle level, observers contend that colleges have become corporatized as higher-education leaders and outsiders increasingly think of students as their customers and education as a commodity or a product that is delivered them. This paradigm of a college education as a transaction has gained strength with the rise of distance education and with colleges' addition of undergraduate and professional degree programs designed to meet expectations from students and their families that a college degree will lead to a job. Many colleges, it should be said, have contributed to these expectations. Ever since economists began talking about the $1-million "wage premium" that college graduates would earn over those with just a high-school degree, college leaders have been touting higher education for its economic payoffs to individuals.

Is the "higher-education industry" attractive to investors?

Education businesses do not attract the kind of money that flows into hot biotechnology or Internet start-ups. But during the first Internet boom, from 1998 to 2001, some fifty for-profit-college companies, along with companies like Blackboard and WebCt, which develop "learning management systems" for web-based courses, caught the attention—and more than $1 billion in capital—from venture-capitalists and other investors. After a fallow five years, investor interest in what is now generally referred to as "Ed-tech" and other education-related ventures perked up again in 2007. And according to GSV Advisors, a merchant bank, from 2007 through 2013, investors poured more than $1.8 billion into some 164 companies related to higher education. Nearly a quarter of that was invested in 2013.[21]

Most of the investor interest now is aimed at companies that claim they have a fix for the things that are "broken" in higher education. The capital has gone to companies like StraighterLine, with its low-cost alternatives to general-education courses, and 2U, which creates partnerships with well-known universities to help them bring degrees online, as well as to ventures like Knewton, a company that uses predictive-analytics technology to personalize the teaching of courses to fit the ways individual students learn best and Copley Retention Systems, which helps college advisors and professors keep students on track to graduate. Investors have also been drawn to companies like Coursera and Udacity, which were both created by Stanford University professors and provide the platforms for massive open online courses, or MOOCs, and to a venture called Minerva, which aims to create a new model of elite higher education that moves its students from city to city over four years. Investors have also backed the company founded in 2012 that runs American Honors, which helps two-year institutions develop the curriculum and related programming for an "honors college" within the community college, and then assist students in transferring to selective four-year colleges to complete their baccalaureate degrees.

Part Four

WHAT'S AHEAD

What does "disruption" mean when it comes to the future of higher education?

In this period of what might be considered higher education's era of the re-set, "disruption" may well be the key buzzword. In the 1990s, Harvard Business School professor Clayton M. Christensen coined the term "disruptive innovation" to describe "a process by which a product or service takes root initially in simple applications at the bottom of a market and then relentlessly moves up market, eventually displacing established competitors." For fifteen years he explained that principle with examples such as mini-mills that made cheap rebar, which upended the business model for giant steel mills, and personal computers, which displaced mainframes.

Sometime around 2011, as traditional colleges found themselves weakened by declines in net tuition and state support, beset by critics for being unaffordable, and judged ill-prepared for the expected wave of minority and low-income students that they had not served well in the past, Christensen and a coterie of others began to warn that those institutions would soon be the latest victims of this kind of disruption. They predicted that for-profit colleges offering greater convenience, and other kind of colleges and providers offering lower-cost degrees via distance-education, like Western Governors' University, would soon have an advantage in the market. These critics began urging colleges to embrace distance education and other approaches to lower college costs and college prices.[1] Christensen, with Henry Eyring, also wrote a book called *The Innovative University*, based heavily on the nontraditional education model used at Brigham Young University-Idaho, where Eyring is a vice president and Christensen's former dean from Harvard, Kim B. Clark, is the president. BYU-Idaho, taking a page from the for-profit-college sector, caters to older students, operates on a year-round calendar, makes extensive use of distance education, and focuses its faculty on teaching rather than research.

Today, "disruptive innovation" has become a catchword and a rallying cry for companies, organizations, policymakers, and in some cases even college trustees themselves who are advocating new and lower-cost approaches to the college experience through nontraditional means (many of which are described in this chapter) and new policies that would allow them to flourish. In circles that do not include those reformers, the term is scorned as shorthand for policies that some say will cheapen higher education—in all senses of the word—by depriving students of opportunities for rich interaction with faculty members and further commodifying higher education. (Of course, this overlooks the fact that because of the "adjunctification" of higher education, many students have long since been missing out on these kinds of interactions, particularly at big institutions.) This faction, who argue that some of the disruptive ideas—technological or otherwise— are inferior to traditional approaches, says they could also weaken higher education by making it easier for lawmakers to cut financial support for traditional education in favor of low-cost alternatives.

It is worth noting that most of the enthusiasm for no-frills, and in many cases untested, disruptive approaches is not aimed at elite institutions and their students, but rather at institutions that enroll large numbers of lower-income and less-prepared students, which may only deepen the divide between higher-education's haves and have-nots—especially if the disruptive approaches prove to be less effective.

What are MOOCs?

Like very few other developments in higher education, massive open online courses, more commonly known as MOOCs, struck a chord in the national consciousness. MOOCs began in 2008 with a two thousand-student University of Manitoba online course taught by Stephen Downes and George Siemens, on "Connectivism and Connected Knowledge," and have since grown exponentially, now making it possible for tens of thousands of students to simultaneously take a course for free from world-renowned professors. Some are for-credit, others just for fun, and they are offered by public, private, and for-profit colleges—and companies—alike. The innovation of MOOCs lies not only in the technology underlying them—the software that allows thousands to participate at once—but also elements like peer-to-peer grading on a mass scale that push the boundaries on pedagogy. Students, policy makers, investors, and news organizations (most famously *The New York Times*, which declared 2012 "the year of the MOOC") quickly became enthralled with the possibilities of using MOOCs to decrease educational costs and reach new audiences of students throughout the world while also building new kinds of learning communities outside the structure of a university.

In fact the idea was not all that new. Since the early 2000s the Massachusetts Institute of Technology and several other universities had been making some (and in the case of MIT's Open Courseware Project, all) course materials freely available. Others, including some of the same professors who created that Duke University MOOC on the history and future of higher education, were also collaborating in a mass way on courses—they call themselves HASTAC for Humanities, Arts,

Science, and Technology Alliance and Collaboratory—albeit not all in an online format. But the MOOCs were able to take advantage of the advances in Internet ubiquity and technology that allowed for simultaneous interaction and better transmission of lectures and other audio-visual features.

In the past few years investors have poured tens of millions into Silicon Valley companies like Coursera and Udacity. The companies provide the technology platforms for displaying MOOC lectures and accompanying tools for sharing course materials, quizzes, class assignments, and the automated or peer grading systems. Both of those big MOOC companies were founded by Stanford University professors (Coursera by Daphne Koller and Andrew Ng; Udacity by Sebastian Thrun). Harvard University and the Massachusetts Institute of Technology then ponied up $60 million to create a third big player in the field, EdX, which is nonprofit and now includes many other major universities as educational and financial partners. Dozens of other platforms and companies soon followed and hundreds of universities announced MOOCs on a host of topics: "Pre-Calculus," "Global Warming: The Science of Climate Change," and "Exploring Beethoven's Piano Sonatas" among them. Most were not for credit, but the American Council on Education has begun a service to evaluate MOOCs seeking such status.

Then in 2013 a backlash began, as reports started to surface about typical drop-out rates higher than 90 percent and poor academic results. Meanwhile, faculty members at some universities began to publicly question whether MOOCs would deprive students of meaningful contact with professors, as well as threaten their very jobs. The most visible of these challenges came from philosophy-department professors at San Jose State University, whose public letter to Harvard's Michael Sandel in the spring of 2013 gave voice to the anxieties many academics were having about MOOCs. Their institution, part of the California State University system, had proposed that they make use of Sandel's MOOC called "Justice." "Let's not kid ourselves; administrations at the CSU are beginning a process of replacing faculty with cheap online education," the public letter said. "Professors who care about public education should not produce products that will replace professors, dismantle departments, and provide a diminished education for students in public universities." (Sandel for his part said he agreed that online courses were no substitute for professors' personal engagement with students, especially in the humanities. "The last thing I want is for my online lectures to be used to undermine faculty colleagues at other universities," he told *The Chronicle of Higher Education*.[2])

As Siemens, the professor who co-taught the first MOOC, put it in a 2014 essay, MOOCs had become "a proxy for our hopes and fears for education." Those hopes and fears persist, in no small part due to faculty members' concerns about who owns the intellectual-property rights to courses they develop into MOOCs and to lingering doubts about how universities and companies like Coursera and Udacity can develop sustainable business models by offering courses for free. (In some cases, students pay a nominal fee if they want a certificate of completion, and colleges can charge students who take MOOCs for credit.) In late 2013, Udacity's founder, Thrun, even told the magazine *Fast Company* that a MOOC may be "a lousy product" to use for educating underprepared students, because they require more structure than the open-access courses offer. And researchers at the University of Pennsylvania found that the majority of its MOOC students were already well-educated, raising further questions about the value of MOOCs to democratize higher education.

While a few skeptics have already begun joking that the acronym really stands for Massively Overhyped Online Courses, some experts still see powerful value in the MOOC phenomenon. For example, they create a trove of data about how students respond to various teaching approaches, which learning scientists at Stanford's Lytics Lab, and researchers elsewhere, are already studying. And as Jeffrey R. Young has noted in

Beyond the MOOC Hype: A Guide to Higher Education's High-Tech Disruption, now that MOOCs can bring superstar lecturers to any campus (or living room) in the world, many professors will be challenged to rethink their own sometimes-stale models of teaching by lecture and PowerPoint.[3]

Are there proposals for new low-cost or even no-cost models of higher education?

With college prices such a point of concern, a few public and private institutions began offering three-year degrees, in some cases only for a limited set of majors, as a way of lowering costs. But that idea has not really caught fire with students, and some educators have questioned the merits of trying to jam four years of college into three. Then in 2011, Texas Governor Rick Perry, a Republican, challenged public colleges in his state to develop bachelor's degree programs that would cost students less than $2,000 a year plus the cost of books. The response was immediate; as Eric Kelderman put it in *The Chronicle of Higher Education*, the idea of a $10,000-degree began spreading "like an Internet meme." Within a year, more than a dozen public colleges in Texas had created such programs, as had all of the public colleges in Florida, where the idea was championed by its Republican Governor, Rick Scott.[4] The term, however, is a bit misleading. In fact, many of these so-called $10,000 degrees depend on students having prior credits, enrolling in low-cost community colleges for part of their course work, or earning credits from online providers offering competency-based assessments.

Of perhaps more significance, the notion that students would pay only $10,000 for a college degree has also raised some larger questions about the value of higher education— a sign of what Thomas Lindsay, director of the Center for Higher Education Policy at the Texas Public Policy Foundation, calls "the growing contempt that students and parents have for higher education," particularly as college leaders have sought to promote the economic value of a degree to individuals rather than emphasizing its inherent merits.[5] The center, a conservative-leaning group which has been influential in Texas politics under Governor Perry, supports the low-cost degrees.

In addition to approaches aimed at cutting down the price for college, some states have been discussing new approaches that would change the way students pay for college in the first place. Oregon, for example, is now studying a "pay it forward" model, under which students would pay no tuition to attend public colleges but agree to pay back 3 percent of their income for twenty years, with the money going into a fund to support future generations of students. The idea grew out of a student project at Portland State University, and students at the University of California at Irvine have proposed a similar tuition model they call "Fix UC." The model has also captured the interest of lawmakers in New Jersey, Ohio, Pennsylvania, and Washington. Some critics, however, note that for students who end up with higher salaries, such an approach would be far more costly than borrowing the money for college and repaying it through the traditional federal student loan program. (There are also several private companies—Lumini, Pave, and Upstart—and at least one community-based nonprofit organization called 13th Avenue, that now offer students similar kinds of income-based repayment options for student loans via arrangements known as "human capital contracts.")

Many of these approaches are based in part on the income-based repayment models for student loans now commonly used in Australia and England. In the United States, income-based repayment options for federal student loans do exist, but they are underused, despite efforts by the Education Department and student advocates to promote them. With such loans, the government absorbs the difference between what was borrowed and what is ultimately paid back.

Another approach to the college-cost issue comes from a cadre of advocates who argue that all public colleges should be made free, with the costs covered by scrapping the existing state and federal tax breaks for such things as 529 College Savings Plans, donations to colleges, and the HOPE and Lifelong Learning tax credits. The idea evokes the era prior to the mid-1970s and early 1980s, when students at the City University of New York and at California public colleges paid no tuition. Robert Samuels, a union leader for University of California lecturers and librarians who makes the case for this approach in his book, *Why Public Higher Education Should Be Free*, argues that it would allow students more freedom to pursue studies that interest them rather than those that they hope will help them get a good-paying job so they can pay off their student-loan debt. He says it could also help reverse the cycle that has made it easier to cut funding for higher education because it is seen as a private rather than a public good.[6] Critics of the idea worry that it would reduce pressure on colleges to find ways to operate more efficiently and less expensively, and that it could increase inequities for lower-income students who might find themselves squeezed out of public colleges by an influx of wealthier students.

In 2014 the free-college idea got a boost from Tennessee Governor William E. Haslam, a Republican, who proposed the Tennessee Promise to give all high school graduates in the state two years of free tuition at a community or technical college. The program, which the legislature adopted, will be financed largely from proceeds from the state's lottery. While some noted that the so-called Tennessee Promise was not as generous as it seemed—the state would still require students to apply for Pell Grants and other student aid and only cover the difference, and as enacted the program will reduce the size of scholarships for freshmen and sophomores at four-year colleges to encourage them to attend community colleges—similar proposals for free community college have also been proposed in Oregon and Mississippi. (In Mississippi the proposal died in a legislative committee in early 2014, but Oregon lawmakers endorsed a plan for the state to formally study the feasibility of the idea.)

What are "open educational resources," and might they reduce college costs?

As we saw in Part One, tuition is not the only cost of going to college. The cost of books and supplies has increased four times the rate of inflation since 1990, according to U.S. Public Interest Research Group, and now averages about $1,200 a year. And despite concern for how it would hurt their grades, more than two-thirds of students say they have skipped buying a book altogether to save money, according to PIRG's recent survey.

In response, some higher-education institutions like Rice University and the Washington State Board for Community & Technical Colleges, companies like Flat World Knowledge and Lumen Learning, and foundations like the Gates, Hewlett, and Twenty Million Minds, have been developing open-course libraries, entire courses, and other programs to promote greater use of free or low-cost materials in place of the textbooks and other materials professors usually assign. Rice, for example, has created a venture called OpenStax College, financed by foundations, to create open-source textbooks that are made available free to students online (and low-cost in print). Its books are already being used by hundreds of colleges. Flat World provides free textbooks and makes its money selling study guides. Lumen, a company created to spur adoption of open resources, is now working with colleges to adopt what it calls its "Textbook Zero" model in which open educational resources would replace all commercial textbooks for every course needed to complete an associate's degree and even the general-education requirements of a bachelor's degree. The movement is not without its skeptics, among them textbook publishers and others who invest in developing, peer-reviewing, and producing new educational content. Such critics question whether a "free" content movement can be financially sustainable while also providing the breadth and depth of resources that academe requires.

Has the "big data" movement made an impact on college teaching and other aspects of higher education?

Just as retail stores have begun corralling mountains of information about their customers to improve services and sales, colleges, too, have begun experimenting with techniques for mining and analyzing data about their students. Higher education's first "big data" junkies were the admissions offices, which often collect data on applicants from the day they first inquire and use it, juxtaposed with other demographic and geographic information, to better predict which applicants will ultimately enroll. They then use that intelligence to focus more recruiting efforts towards such applicants. Now, colleges, companies, and others are adopting some of the techniques for a wider variety of purposes that hold promise for improving student outcomes.

Arizona State University, for example, tracks and monitors data on how its students are performing in courses they need for their majors, whether they're checking in regularly with their academic advisors, and even whether their financial aid is in order, all with the goal of keeping students on track toward their degrees. Students who fare poorly in prerequisites are sometimes encouraged to consider other majors. Purdue University, meanwhile, has created Course Signals, based on similar principles but designed to inform students in real time (with red, yellow, or green lights on their course homepage) how they're doing in a particular class and to spur instructors to intervene. Its system is now being marketed by Ellucian, a major software company in higher education.

Other companies that sell learning-management systems offer comparable products. And Austin Peay State University, in Tennessee, created DegreeCompass software to suggest courses for students based on their transcripts, much in the way Amazon recommends products to its customers. A company called Desire2Learn bought it in 2013 with plans to expand it as a service to include degree and career selection options as well.

Truth be told, most of these efforts are not "big data" projects in the way that the term is understood in industry or complex and data-rich research projects because they do not involve all that much information. But for higher education, they represent a sea change.

Data analytics and predictive technologies are also crucial to burgeoning developments in personalized educational offerings that experts hope will someday become more pervasive and lead to improvements in student learning and lower costs. Companies like Knewton, which works with publishers and others to embed "adaptive-learning" features into digital courses, are on the forefront of this movement. So too is the Open Learning Initiative, the grant-funded project at Carnegie Mellon that spends $500,000 to $1 million per course to create courses based on deep research in learning science. The courses—including "Introduction to Chemistry" and a mini-course called "Arabic for Global Exchange"—are available for free to other colleges and individuals.

What are "badges" and "stackable credentials"? Might they replace traditional college credentials?

For centuries, the college degree was the currency that society looked to as the measure of academic accomplishment. That monopoly on this kind of societal "signaling," however, may be starting to crumble. Fueled by tales of grade inflation and their own disappointments with the underwhelming communication and reasoning skills of young college graduates, some employers and others are now questioning what a college degree really signifies. At the same time, the rise of alternative-educational models continue to open up opportunities for students to learn outside the confines of a traditional accredited university, and they want a way to telegraph evidence of those accomplishments to others.

Badges, which have already been put into use by some colleges and other educational organizations, are often likened to the patches earned by Boy and Girl Scouts or the points earned by winning video games. They are a way of recognizing students' specific accomplishments or skills and communicating them to a broader audience in a way that traditional transcripts do not. The badges movement falls within a broader effort to develop tools for students to create and transmit personal educational portfolios that reflect not only their courses and grades, but also what they have learned from, say, a Khan Academy or Lynda.com video.

Proponents of these badges include the Gates and Mozilla Foundations, the latter of which has sponsored contests to develop common technological standards for how such badges can be shared over the Internet. It also includes companies like Degreed, which provides an online platform to display certificates and badges of completion in a "digital lifelong diploma," and Parchment, which handles electronic transfer of credentials but is pushing for colleges to begin offering a standardized and digital "postsecondary achievement report" that would also reflect students' co-curricular accomplishments. Although the idea is still relatively new, it does have its fans, among them, the former president of Harvard University, Derek Bok, who says traditional transcripts are a weak tool for communicating what students have learned. With the addition of badges, on the other hand, students could more easily flesh out their experience to employers and others, says Bok—although he has also warned that colleges need to be careful about letting others define the meaning of a college credential.

"It would be a mistake," he said, "for universities to let others take over the task of explaining what your students know."[7]

Some colleges, like New York University, Purdue University, and the University of California at Davis, have already begun using badges. At NYU, the School of Professional and Continuing Studies offered a digital badge to every student who had received a certificate since 1990; about a quarter accepted and most are now displaying them on LinkedIn or some other social-media platforms. UC-Davis, meanwhile, took the badges idea beyond simple branding and used it to help rethink and re-make a degree program, breaking down the various skills and competencies taught as part of that degree. Now students studying Sustainable Agriculture and Food Systems can earn badges showing their prowess in subjects like "systems thinking."

The badges movement has also helped highlight the need for ways to better recognize educational credentials short of a degree that have value in their own right, whether acquired from a college, the military, or in the workplace. Some of these credentials can lead to promotions and higher pay. And when pieced together in a logical sequence, they also can be stepping stones to a degree. Supporters of such "stackable credentials" are now urging colleges to create more formal pathways to degrees based on such credentials.

Though still in its infancy, the badges movement could have a disruptive effect on higher education. Advocates for badges say they have the potential to replace some of the advantages now enjoyed by graduates of more-elite colleges—gained on the reputation of their colleges and not necessarily their own achievements—with a more meritocratic system. As put by Michael Moe, co-founder of the investment firm GSV Advisors, badges reflect "what you know versus where you go." Yet as Parchment's founder Matthew Pittinsky has warned, the "un-college" movement that has helped give rise to badges also has the potential to "exacerbate inequality," particularly for students coming from less-educated homes. For many such students, Pittinsky has noted, it can be hard enough just to navigate college, never mind finding and bundling together the right courses "in a world of infinite options."

What are competency-based degrees, and is there momentum behind them?

As the name suggests, competency-based degrees are awarded to students based on whether they have mastered the material rather than how long they attended college and how many "seat time" credits they've earned. The concept is not new to higher education. Many colleges, including public universities like Charter Oak State College in Connecticut, have a mechanism for awarding some credit to students based on an assessment of their prior knowledge. And for years, institutions like DePaul University's School for Learning in Illinois and the online Western Governors University have allowed students to earn degrees by demonstrating their mastery of a series of specific competencies, in some cases based on courses they've taken on their own. But the approach has not been widespread, because many colleges still see it as their job to teach students and because the awarding of federal student-aid has been geared around policies that use the "credit hour" to allocate grants and loans. (Cynics might also say that colleges have not embraced it because it is harder to charge students for what seems like a do-it-yourself degree.)

Recently, as policymakers, foundations, and students have begun pushing for more-convenient and less-expensive alternatives to the traditional college experience, and as more adults with on-the-job and life experience have been starting or returning to college, competency-based degrees have become a favored idea. The New American Foundation, the Center for American Progress, and the Lumina Foundation are among the approach's most vocal supporters. In 2013 Southern New Hampshire University became the first institution to win formal approval from the U.S. Department of

Education for its new College for America to offer federal student aid to students who undergo "direct assessment" to measure what they've learned. (Prior to that, institutions offering competency-based degrees either did not use financial aid or they did so by creating credit-hour equivalencies for the subject matter and assessments they offered.) Programs like the one by College for America, which recruits students with the promise of "No Courses, No Grades, No Instructors," have attracted working adults who appreciate the self-paced approach of competency-based education.

Northern Arizona University, a public institution, and the for-profit Capella University have also received federal approval to offer such degrees. The University of Wisconsin system was also an early adopter with its Flex degrees, but those competency-based degrees are still linked to the credit-hour standard. Although some colleges and faculty still harbor doubts about the rigor of such programs, many others are beginning to explore competency-based programs and have begun urging the Department of Education to develop more avenues for expanding student-aid eligibility for them.

What other alternative-education options are there for earning college credits?

For those inclined toward an educational approach that the author Anya Kamenetz has dubbed "DIY U," options are expanding. Along with StraighterLine, the company mentioned previously that provides self-paced, low-cost, general-education courses available through agreements with colleges, a few other free-standing companies and organizations have begun to offer courses as well. One of them, a venture owned by Capella called Sophia, requires students to complete a series of challenges and milestones within sixty days to earn the course credits. The classes can qualify for credit because they have been approved by the College Credit Recommendation Service operated by the American Council on Education. Others, which are provided free by the Saylor Foundation, are eligible for credit through the National College Credit Recommendation Service, which operates under the auspices of the New York State Board of Regents. The Saylor courses, which involve no professors or mentors, rely heavily on materials that are freely available on the Internet, like Khan Academy videos and material published under open-source licenses, and are developed by subject experts hired by the foundation.

This alt-ed movement is still in the early stages and is likely to take on a variety of shapes. For example, Rob Skiff, a Vermont entrepreneur behind a fledgling venture called Oplerno, is trying to develop what he calls "a self-organizing, nonlinear, complex adaptive system," built around adjunct professors who propose their own courses and prices and then get to keep 80 to 90 percent of what the students pay in tuition. Another more established venture is the University of the People, founded by an Israeli distance-education company pioneer named Shai Reshef. It depends entirely on volunteer professors and deans from around the world to provide online degrees that are essentially free. The university builds its classes on open-educational resources and an Internet course platform that does not require rich broadband capacity, so the degrees can be accessible to students in places like rural Africa and earthquake-ravaged areas of Haiti. (Students, who come from more than 140 countries, are asked to pay $10 to $50 to apply and then $100 per exam, if they have the money.) Although designed primarily for students in the developing world, about a quarter of its seven hundred students were based in the United States when it became accredited and graduated its first eight students in 2014. With accreditation, it hopes to have five thousand students by 2016.

It is hard to know how credits and degrees earned through Saylor, StraighterLine, and others will ultimately be regarded. Proponents contend that the more these alternative approaches catch on—and perhaps the more ideas like badges take root—the more acceptable they may become. Already, more than one-fifth of all college graduates complete their degree at an institution other than the one where they started, and as Jeffrey J. Selingo describes in *College UnBound: The Future of Higher Education and What It Means for Students*, increasingly this "student swirl" is expanding to include nontraditional providers.[8] Yet it is also the case that the many investors and reformers advocating for such alternative models are themselves the products of elite universities with MBAs from Harvard and Wharton.

Are American colleges adopting a German model of apprenticeships?

The attention and money now focused on MOOCs, competency-based degrees, and big data have overshadowed changes in postsecondary education that are not built around technology. Yet in some states, most notably in the Carolinas, which are home to several German-owned manufacturing plants, and at Ivy Tech Community College in Indiana, officials have developed programs to better link college offerings with factory apprenticeship programs akin to those more commonly found in Northern Europe. The efforts, many of them funded by companies like BMW and Siemens, help the companies develop the workers they need to operate the advanced robotics of the modern factory. They also address the needs of high-school graduates who are not interested in college but face an economy where many of the jobs require postsecondary schooling.

Apprenticeships are still a small factor in the economy and the higher-education landscape. According to the Center on American Progress, America had 358,000 active registered apprentices in 2012—only 7 percent of the number of apprenticeships in England when adjusting for population size.[9] But the center, which advocates for expansion of such programs through tax breaks for companies that provide them and other incentives, is among several groups urging colleges to help develop them as an alternative to their traditional college offerings. It notes that by 2020, projections say the nation will face a shortage of three million workers with associate's degrees or higher and five million workers with technical certificates and credentials. The center also points to studies showing that workers who take part in apprenticeships will make as much as $300,000 more in their lifetimes than those without the opportunity—a figure that is smaller than the oft-cited $1-million wage premium for a bachelor's degree, but nonetheless a value in the marketplace.

So does all this emphasis on career-focused degrees spell doom for a traditional liberal arts education?

Liberal arts colleges are dying. But that has been the case for decades. And it does not necessarily mean that the values and principles of a liberal-arts education are on the wane. These colleges, which include some, like Amherst College and Colgate University, that date from the 1800s and are quite traditional, and others that gained attention for pushing the envelope on educational innovation in the 1960s, share some commonalties. They're typically private and residential, enroll 800 to 2,500 students, concentrate on nonprofessional majors in the arts, sciences, and humanities, and emphasize small classes where students are taught by professors, not graduate teaching assistants. Many began as religiously affiliated institutions and remain focused on undergraduates.

But the term is not exact, so much so that in 1990, when the higher-education scholar David W. Breneman surveyed the traits of six hundred institutions then presumed to be liberal arts colleges, he concluded that in reality there were probably no more than 212 that truly fit the bill. Many of the colleges he eliminated were those that had added graduate and professional schools, or that awarded more than 60 percent of their undergraduate degrees in "professional" majors such as education or business. Twenty-two years later, a team of scholars applied the same criteria to Breneman's list of 212 and found only 130 institutions that would still qualify.[10]

That decline, along with other trends—like students' preference for majors in business, engineering, and nursing (more than half of all undergraduates major in one of those areas) and evidence that at least at the "best" liberal arts colleges, enrollments do not reflect the diversity of the college student population (judging by Pell Grant enrollments)—has prompted some to question whether the colleges are losing their relevance, becoming in the words of one foundation official, "too boutiquey."[11]

At the same time, however, an increasing number of colleges, not just small four-year institutions but community colleges and larger publics, have begun embracing a curricular and teaching model called "liberal learning," which emphasizes the critical thinking, analysis, communications, and visual-literacy skills that a traditional liberal-arts education aims to provide. In our fast-changing economy, such skills are also the ones that employers say they value most and that college graduates later in life say are most valuable to them. And while engineering majors still earn more money, a recent analysis of Census Bureau data also shows that undergraduates in the humanities and social sciences eventually earned more than those who majored in a professional or pre-professional field like accounting or nursing.[12]

The 1,200-member American Association of Colleges & Universities has become the most visible champion of this approach, arguing that liberal learning, which includes broad knowledge "and a strong sense of value, ethics, and civic engagement," could and should take place at any kind of college, not only small private ones. (The skills are also increasingly valued overseas, particularly at universities in Taiwan, South Korea, Hong Kong, and China, where university leaders, often with help from American educators, have been trying to foster the personalized approach of a liberal arts education, even as some American institutions shift to a more industrial-ized model.) Advocates also note that relative to their share of the employed population, liberal arts graduates dispropor-tionally pursued careers in social service sectors, further sug-gesting the importance of a liberal arts education as a social and individual good.

How widespread is distance education, and how is it evolving?

As we've seen throughout this book, distance education, most of which occurs online, is a growing piece of the higher-education landscape—but it is not quite as widespread as some previous studies had estimated. According to estimates drawn from newly published U.S. Department of Education data, a quarter of all students—about 5.35 million—took at least one course that was exclusively or partly offered as a distance edu-cation course in fall 2012. Other estimates had previously put that figure as high as seven million. Of those 5.35 million, some two million undergraduates (11 percent of all undergraduates) and another 650,000 graduate students (22 percent of the total of that group) were enrolled in at least one course considered "exclusively" distance education. As previously mentioned, not every distance-education student is an exclusively online student, as some participate in low-residency or credit-by-exam programs, or with other technologies.

For both graduate and undergraduate programs, the most common courses and degrees offered via distance education are those in business, marketing, computer- and information-technologies, and health-related fields. A number of colleges also run thriving online programs offering mas-ter's degrees and graduate-level certificates in education—pro-grams that are attractive to working teachers who often can receive a bump in pay for having such credentials.

As of fall 2012, more than two thousand colleges and campuses were offering distance education to at least fifty students. That suggests that there are many colleges with further ambitions to expand distance education, according to distance-education expert Richard Garrett. Yet as Garrett has also noted, when it comes to institutions currently making extensive use of online education, the numbers are far smaller. Indeed for online programs considered fully online, just twenty institutions command more than a third of the market. He has also noted that, the name aside, a healthy portion of so-called distance learning is rather local. About half of the students enrolled in courses considered exclusively distance education reside in the same state as the institution offering the course. Some of them are even residential students at the college who just prefer to take the class online.[13]

For-profit colleges are still the biggest players in distance education. Thirteen of those twenty institutions with the most students enrolled in fully-online programs were for-profits, according to the Department of Education's fall 2012 data analyzed by Garrett. The University of Phoenix, then with more than 250,000 online students, and Ashford University, with nearly 77,000, topped the list, although online and other enrollments there and at other for-profit colleges have since plunged in the wake of rising questions about the sector. (The other for-profit leaders in online education, in order of their enrollments, were: American Public University System; Walden, Kaplan, and, DeVry Universities; Everest institutes, owned by Corinthian Colleges Inc.; Capella, Grand Canyon, and Strayer Universities; Colorado Technical University, owned by Career Education Corp.; and Columbia Southern and Full Sail Universities.)

Among all public and private nonprofit universities, Liberty University, a Christian liberal arts university founded in 1971 by the evangelist Jerry Falwell, is far-and-away the leader; it is third overall, with nearly sixty-two thousand exclusively online students. Other nonprofit institutions in the top twenty are Western Governors University; Excelsior College, an adult-focused online institution; University of Maryland University College; Thomas Edison State College, an adult-focused public

college in New Jersey; Rio Salado College, a community college in Arizona, and Ivy Tech in Indiana.

The number of college leaders who say distance education is critical to their institutions' long-term strategy has
been growing, but many of their faculty members continue
to doubt its effectiveness compared to face-to-face teaching.
A study conducted by the Babson Survey Research Group
and *Inside Higher Ed* found that nearly four out of ten professors doubt it has the potential to be as effective as traditional
classes.[14]

It is significant, then, that the majority of online students are those taking courses where only a portion of their
studies takes place at a distance. Such courses, known as
"hybrid" or "blended learning" courses, offer some of the
convenience and cost-savings of fully online courses with
some of the presumed benefits of face-to-face teaching. Fully
online degrees are likely to grow, particularly in the post-
baccalaureate and adult-student markets. But it is these
hybrid versions of online education—cousins to the teaching trend known as the "flipped classroom" where students
watch pre-recorded lectures from a distance and use their
class time to engage more directly with their professors and
classmates—that are more likely to gain acceptance at the
colleges that cater to more of what used to be considered
traditional students.

Indeed, online education is already growing in stature and
acceptance as more public and nonprofit colleges have begun
to embrace it, either with their own resources or in conjunc-
tion with third-party companies. That includes a few institutions that often top the rankings lists for selectivity. In fact,
one distance-education enabler company, the previously
mentioned 2U, now works only with top-ranked colleges, like
the University of Southern California for graduate programs
in education and the University of North Carolina at Chapel
Hill for graduate programs in business. At the same time 2U's

efforts to offer distance education through a consortium of leading undergraduate residential colleges fell apart in 2014 after less than a year.

Will online education eventually make campuses obsolete?

Physical campuses are safe for the foreseeable future. But judging by some of the innovations already taking root—a football field turned into an organic farm at tiny Paul Quinn College in Dallas, the town-gown collaboration of the Oberlin Project to remake the Ohio town and the namesake college into an interconnected, self-sustainable community—more colleges in the future may be using their campuses and their physical presence in the community in different and more intentionally educational ways.

The grandest college campuses are places of inspiration, with iconic architecture and public spaces, like The Lawn at the University of Virginia, the colonnades along the quadrangle at Stanford University, and the domed Low Library of Columbia University. But even those that are not as architecturally or aesthetically lauded still hold significant value, providing not just the classroom and laboratories of formal education but the opportunity for students to interact more casually with their professors. They also offer students the shared social space with their peers for the "lateral learning" that is so prized a part of the experience of a college education. (Columbia University's Andrew Delbanco offers a tribute to the value of such learning, as well as the opportunity for self-discovery, intellectual growth, and other hard-to-quantify benefits of higher education in his book, *College: What It Was, Is, and Should Be*.)

Campuses are also important to the social and economic fabrics of the communities in which they are located, in no small part because they are sources of culture and are the kinds of employers that are not likely to suddenly uproot one day to a locale where labor costs are lower or the tax breaks are better. In some small towns, especially in the Midwest, the community would hardly exist without the college. And in some cases, most notably at Syracuse and Portland State Universities, institutions have shifted curriculum and research so it centers more on the real-world issues of importance to the communities where they are located.

The economic value of college campuses can matter so much to communities, in fact, that a few of them have gone to great lengths to bring colleges in. Since 2012, for example, the city of Mesa, Arizona, has managed to lure five out-of-state institutions—Albright College and A.T. Still, Benedictine, Upper Iowa, and Wilkes Universities—to establish branch campuses within its environs. In 2014, the city of Carlsbad, California, set up a booth at a higher-education conference in San Diego, hoping to find a university willing to build a graduate-engineering school in the city limits. And on a far bigger scale, New York City, already rich with colleges and great universities, recently landed what is expected to be a $2-billion, applied-sciences campus jointly run by Cornell University and Technion-Israel Institute of Technology on Roosevelt Island. The city so valued the current and future economic benefits of a physical campus in science and engineering that it established a contest to attract bidders and offered $100 million in city assistance to the winner in 2011.

Campuses also seem to matter to students, even if they do not attend in person. Consider that two of the biggest for-profit colleges, Ashford and Grand Canyon Universities—in Clinton, Iowa and Phoenix, Arizona, respectively—quite pointedly highlight their physical campuses in the marketing and recruiting materials, even though residential students make up just a small fraction of their overall enrollments. The same kind of thinking assists nonprofit colleges in improving their appeal to online students, many of whom regard the existence of a robust physical campus as a sign that they are enrolling in a "real" college.

And as the investment in the applied-sciences campus on Roosevelt Island in New York City suggests, many still recognize the value of grouping researchers and professors together in a shared space. Distance education has promise, and professors can and do certainly collaborate on research online. But the intellectual and economic synergies that have helped to create Silicon Valley and the high-tech and biomedical hubs around Boston and Austin, for example, arose from the concentration of facilities and the community of academic talent that only major college campuses can provide.

Just as many institutions have overhauled their libraries, making them less places for storing books and more into locations where students can study and socialize together (Goucher College's Athenaeum library, opened in 2009, includes a coffee bar, an art gallery, computer labs, and an exercise area), college leaders are reconsidering how to better use the rest of their campus—and its environs—to reinforce educational goals and operate them more efficiently. For example, many of the new academic buildings are designed with more flexible space, to accommodate students working on projects in teams. And, mindful of the ballooning costs of maintaining buildings, a few colleges, including big institutions, have already begun to rethink the very shape of their campuses. Ohio State University, for one, has adopted a "no new net space" policy, and the University of Massachusetts at Amherst plans to tear down older and obsolete buildings and replace them with smaller, more efficient structures. Although colleges in general are notorious for inefficient use of the facilities, with campuses sitting idle over summers, vacation breaks, and even Fridays, in recent years increasing numbers of colleges have tried to redress those failings by scheduling more classes on nights and weekends, and expanding their calendars to something closer to a year-round schedule.

Going a step further, some sixty residential colleges have partially converted their campuses into homes for "low-residency" programs. Such programs are typically designed for working adults who undertake most of their courses as independent study or distance-education from their homes and then gather with classmates and faculty on campus once or several times a year for more intensive instruction, discussion, and feedback. Goddard College, an institution that has been experimental in focus (and often on the edge financially) since its founding in 1938, became fully low-residency in the early 2000s and now enrolls about eight hundred students.

Several colleges have also begun working more directly with outside parties when developing facilities. In some cases, as with the many residence halls and apartment complexes recently constructed on college campus in collaboration with private developers, the partnerships let colleges devote less of their own capital to buildings. In other cases, the collaborations effectively extend the campus to include other major cultural institutions. Such was the case for Drexel University, when it absorbed Philadelphia's Academy of Natural Sciences in 2011, and for George Washington University, which the same year began plans to take over the Washington, D.C. Textile Museum and in 2014 announced it would absorb the Corcoran School of Art + Design, including its landmark Beaux Arts building. In each case, the universities said they would add academic programs to make use of the new artistic and scientific resources. And while arrangements of this scope are hardly common, they do reflect the thinking that many college leaders now espouse about "doubling down" on their campuses with investments that more closely tie the facilities to the academic mission.

To be sure, however, campuses can also be a financial drain, and colleges where enrollments are falling may well be looking to shed excess real-estate in the years to come, just as the National Labor College sought to do with its forty-seven-acre campus near Washington, D.C. in 2013. Like that college, which closed before it could reap the financial benefits of the sale, not all of them, especially those in rural locations, will be successful in doing so.

CONCLUSION

Should we be optimistic about the future of higher education in America?

In May 2014, Gallup reported results of the first of five planned annual surveys on the state of American college graduates. The landmark survey found that compared to the population as a whole, those who had finished college seemed more content in their careers and more satisfied with their lives than those who had not. Good news for colleges. But this Gallup-Purdue Index also identified strong variations in graduates' feelings about how lives were affected by their college experiences. Graduates who felt they had had professors who cared about them, had a mentor during their time in college, and had internships or work opportunities that applied to what they were learning were far more likely later in life to be engaged in their careers and have higher overall well-being compared to those who disagreed with those statements.

Developers of the Gallup-Purdue Index said the findings showed that *how* students attend college may be more important than where they go or what major they choose. Just as important in this era of doubt about the value college, the findings suggest that a college that chooses to ensure that it has provided these and similarly significant experiences can be pretty certain that it will have a meaningful impact on the lives of its students and their families.

In American higher education today, the future belongs to those kinds of choosers, to the institutions that take steps to ensure and demonstrate that what they offer and how they offer it makes a difference. So whether to be optimistic about that future is really a question of whether colleges have the vision to recognize their own particular challenges and the wherewithal to adapt.

Many can and will. Yet even if they can take on the problems of their own making—bureaucracies run amok or sacred cows like intercollegiate athletics—they face an uphill fight. Not only is the societal schism between rich and poor reflected in the demographics of higher education enrollment, colleges themselves face a similar and growing rich–poor divide as institutions. In a country that is growing more and more urbanized, many of the most vulnerable institutions are small colleges in rural locations, and no doubt in the next few years, a number of them, and others, will fold at a faster pace than ever before. And with the stagnation and uncertainty of the U.S. (and global) economy still weighing heavily on many families, and many others still mired in real poverty, few, if any, colleges will escape the struggle of finding the money to make their education affordable. Colleges hoping for some big new infusion of government support will surely be disappointed.

At the same time, the pressures from organizations, from government, and from investors and businesses to reshape the very nature of college under the banner of innovation holds both promise and peril. The promise lies in the potential for new approaches that are more cost-effective, more creative, and more suitable for today's students. The peril is that what results could be (or may already be) a more commodified and less-enriching version of higher education—a faster and cheaper "college lite" for students who are not wealthy or sophisticated enough to make another choice. The places where MOOCs, or subsequent innovations, replace professors will not be the Ivy League colleges and similarly elite institutions. If there is a hollowing out in higher education it is more likely to happen at community colleges, regional state universities, for-profits, and other institutions that provide most of the educational opportunity for low-income and lower-middle class students. That makes it all the more crucial that those involved in shaping the future of higher education take seriously the question, Reinvention for whom?

Yet as the previous chapters note, there are also reasons for hope: While colleges may chafe at the accountability pressures, for example, the movement is also beginning to push institutions to focus more on matters like improving student retention and student learning. One sign of the latter: four hundred or so colleges are now working with the Degree Qualifications Profile, a Lumina Foundation–backed effort to create common reference points that define the intellectual skills students should develop while earning an associate bachelor's, or master's degree. In an environment where higher education is sometimes thought of as a product to be delivered, it is efforts like that and others, which aim to reclaim the special nature of higher education, that show the sector's resilience. Meanwhile, income-based repayment programs for student loans, and perhaps soon even for tuition directly, could ease some students' concerns about college costs. And certainly the focus on cost containment and the attention to shifting population patterns is prompting more than a few colleges to think smarter about how they spend their administrative dollars and where they go to recruit students. It's no surprise, then, that more and more colleges from the Northeast and the Midwest are now scouting high schools in the Southwest.

Pundits often analogize higher education to industries that have disappeared from the business landscape, but that comparison may not give colleges enough credit for some of their built-in advantages: the centuries of tradition and experience from which to draw upon and the very smart people on their payrolls.

What will it take for colleges to survive and thrive? For starters, focus and vigilance will be vital. Cruise-control leadership at colleges just won't cut it, and institutions where presidents and trustees act otherwise will learn that lesson the hard way. Philanthropy will matter more than ever, particularly for costs like financial aid. And even in the Internet era, the campus will matter too, be it a Harvard Yard or the brightly lit floor of a suburban office park building, its glow visible from the highway interchange as University of Phoenix students within meet face-to-face with their accounting instructor.

In his 1989 book *The Great Good Place*, author Ray Oldenberg describes the value of "third places," those locations in our society that are neither home nor work that people seek out to find community and engagement. Writ large, campuses are "work" places for the people employed there and, in effect, for the students. But the value of campuses, in history and to the future, lies especially as venues for those all-important "third places." They are the home to the recreation centers, the dining halls, the libraries, the arts centers that, to paraphrase Oldenberg, help to both create human community and celebrate it. Campuses, like colleges, are vastly different from each other. And in all likelihood they, like colleges, are headed for big changes. But for the most part, campuses are enduring—and in much the same way, it is safe to say, so, too, is higher education.

ACKNOWLEDGMENTS

Writing is a solitary undertaking, but as I have come to learn, one doesn't write a book without a lot of help. I owe thanks in many directions.

As a reporter at *The Chronicle of Higher Education* for twenty-six years, I've been privileged to know many of the country's most thoughtful experts on higher education. The work of many of them has informed my reporting for this book, but I especially thank Tony Carnevale and Jeff Strohl at Georgetown University, Susan Fitzgerald at Moody's, Richard Garrett at i-graduate, Mark Kantrowitz at Edvisors, Rita Kirshstein at AIR, Robert Lytle and Jesse Tau at the Parthenon Group, Tom Mortenson at the Pell Institute, and Jane Wellman, all-around wise person, for making the time to explain their research, share their insights, and answer my many questions.

I could not have started or sustained this project without the counsel of Scott Manning, Randy Auerbach (whose "tech support" also bailed me out more often than I should admit), Jeff Selingo, and Vicki Stearn. Thanks, also, to my brothers Sam and Larry Blumenstyk—Sam for his ever-present support and Larry for his support and for lending the expertise of Learning Associates to this endeavor.

I am also lucky to have a day job that is one of the greatest in journalism today. *The Chronicle* is a terrific place to work, thanks in no small part to the many smart, creative, talented, and generous people who are now, and have been, my colleagues. I could never have written this book without all the work they do each day. I particularly thank Liz McMillen, *The Chronicle's* editor, for encouraging me to pursue this project; Lee Gardner, my immediate editor, for his patience during my many absences; Ron Coddington, for putting style into the book's graphical elements; and Corbin Gwaltney, *The Chronicle's* founder, for creating a news organization that has nurtured me and so many others.

I owe an enormous debt of gratitude to my *Chronicle* colleague Scott Carlson, my former editor Marty van der Werf, and Professor John Thelin of the University of Kentucky, all of whom read the manuscript in an earlier form and offered valuable critiques. Any errors of fact or interpretation, however, are mine.

Tim Bent and Keely Latcham of Oxford University Press approached me about writing a book about the "crisis" in higher education in early 2013. Despite my hesitation over the premise (hence the question mark in the title), every day since then I have grown more and more appreciative of the opportunity they gave me to step back from my daily and weekly reporting on colleges to take stock of the sector from a different perspective. I am especially grateful to Keely, whose thoughtful and graceful edits—from the proposal stage to the final draft—improved my work at every step.

Finally, I thank two people who will never see this book: my parents Adele and Victor Blumenstyk, who died in the late 1990s. They were teenagers in Poland when the Nazis invaded and never had the chance to finish high school, much less go to college. But they survived concentration camps and the war, met each other, came to America and learned English, and proudly sent me and my brothers to college and professional school. Even though they experienced higher education only through their children, they believed in its power and in the opportunities that America offered. Those beliefs live on in me, and of course, in countless others. If this book helps to inform the debate about the future of higher education in America, as I hope it does, it will also honor their memory.

Washington, D.C.

June 2014

NOTES

Author's Note

1. "Unequal Family Income and Unequal Educational Opportunity 1970 to 2012," Thomas G. Mortenson, *Postsecondary Education Opportunity*, Pell Institute for the Study of Opportunity in Higher Education, October, 2013.

Introduction

1. "Current Term Enrollment Report: Fall 2013," National Student Clearinghouse Research Center, December, 2013.

2. The 1970 book, *The New Depression in Higher Education*, is one sign of that concern. It is the product of a study of colleges' financial health, undertaken by Earl F. Cheit, at the behest of the Carnegie Commission; *The Overeducated American* was published in 1976.

3. Based on statistics gathered by The Pell Institute on seat-belt use (from the American Journal of Public Health), on obesity (from the National Center for Health Statistics), on cigarette use (from the Center for Disease Control and Prevention), on voting rates (from the U.S. Census Bureau), on reading (from the National Endowment for the Arts), and on volunteerism rates (from the Bureau of Labor Statistics); Conclusions on taxes come from numerous reports including "A Well-Educated Workforce Is Key to State Prosperity," Noah Berger and Peter Fisher, Economic Policy Institute, August 22, 2013.

4. "Failure to Launch: Structural Shift and the New Lost Generation," Anthony P. Carnevale, Andrew R. Hanson, and Artem Gulish, Center on Education and the Workforce, Georgetown University and The Generations Initiative, September 2013. https://cew.georgetown.edu/failuretolaunch.

5. "The College Payoff: Education, Occupation, Lifetime Earnings," Anthony P. Carnevale, Stephen J. Rose, and Ban Cheah, Center on Education and the Workforce, Georgetown University, August 5, 2011. http://cew.georgetown.edu/collegepayoff.

6. "Career and Technical Education: Five Ways that Pay" Anthony P. Carnevale, Tamara Jayasundera, and Andrew R. Hanson, Center on Education and the Workforce, Georgetown University, September 2012. http://cew.georgetown.edu/ctefiveways.

7. "Education Pays, 2013: The Benefits of Higher Education for Individuals and Society," Sandy Baum, Jennifer Ma, Kathleen Payea, The College Board, 2013. http://trends.collegeboard.org/sites/default/files/education-pays-2013-full-report.pdf.

8. The unemployment rate is 3.9 percent for college graduates, versus 7.5 percent for high-school graduates at the time of this writing.

9. "The Rising Cost of *Not* Going to College," Pew Research Center, February 11, 2014.

10. Report from Burning Glass, February 5, 2014.

11. "Education Pays, 2013."

12. "New Year, Same Bad News for Recent College Grads," Andrew P. Kelly, American Enterprise Institutes Ideas blog, January 7, 2014.

13. Based on calculations from the College Board and the U.S. Bureau of Labor Statistics.

14. "The American Freshman: National Norms 2013," Kevin Eagan, Jennifer B. Lozano, Sylvia Hurtado, Matthew H. Case, Cooperative Institutional Research Program, Higher Education Research Institute, University of California at Los Angeles, March 2014. http://www.heri.ucla.edu/monographs/TheAmericanFreshman2013.pdf.

15. "Where A Is Ordinary: The Evolution of American College and University Grading," 1940–2009, Stuart Rojstaczer and Christopher Healy, *Teachers College Record,* Volume 114, Number 7, 2012.

16. "The Role of Higher Education in Career Development: Employer Perceptions," Survey by American Public Media's *Marketplace* and *The Chronicle of Higher Education,* December, 2012.

17. "Why Accredit Colleges and Universities that (New Data Show) Aren't Delivering?" Mark S. Schneider, The Quick & the Ed blog, January 10, 2014.

18. "State Investment and Disinvestment in Higher Education, FY 1961 to FY 2014," Thomas G. Mortenson, *Postsecondary Educational Opportunity,* February, 2014.

Part One

1. "American Adults Better Educated Than Ever Before," Pew Research Center, January 10, 2013.

2. Data on students' part-time status are based on Fall 2012 enrollment figures drawn from the *Digest of Education Statistics,* Table 303.70; other data in the paragraph were compiled in "Yesterday's Nontraditional Student Is Today's Traditional Student," by the Center for Postsecondary and Economic Success, June 29, 2011.

3. "Fast Facts: Enrollment," National Center for Education Statistics, U.S. Department of Education, http://nces.ed.gov/fastfacts/display.asp?id=98 (accessed May 25, 2014) and "Total fall enrollment in degree-granting institutions, by attendance status, sex, and age: Selected years, 1970 through 2021," Digest of Education Statistics, Table 224, http://nces.ed.gov/programs/digest/d12/tables/dt12_224.asp (accessed May 24, 2014).

4. "Total fall enrollment in degree-granting postsecondary institutions, by level of enrollment, sex, attendance status, and race/ethnicity of student: Selected years, 1976 through 2012," Digest of Education Statistics, 2013 Tables and Figures, Table 306.10,

http://nces.ed.gov/programs/digest/d13/tables/dt13_306.10.asp (accessed May 25, 2014).

5. "Among Recent High School Grads, Hispanic College Enrollment Rate Surpasses that of Whites," Mark Hugo Lopez, Pew Research Center, September 4, 2013; http://www.pewresearch.org/fact-tank/2013/09/04/hispanic-college-enrollment-rate-surpasses-whites-for-the-first-time/ (accessed May 27, 2014) and Digest of Education Statistics, 2013 Tables and Figures, Table 306.10.

6. Digest of Education Statistics, 2013 Tables and Figures, Table 306.10.

7. "Degrees conferred by degree-granting institutions, by level of degree and sex of student: Selected years, 1869–70 through 2020," Digest of Educational Statistics, 2011, Table 283, http://nces.ed.gov/programs/digest/d11/tables/dt11_283.asp?referrer=report (accessed May 25, 2014).

8. In fall 2012, there were about 11.7 million women enrolled in all sectors and all levels of higher education, versus 8.9 million men, "Total fall enrollment in degree-granting postsecondary institutions, by attendance status, sex of student, and control of institution: Selected years, 1947 through 2012," Digest of Education Statistics Table 303.10, http://nces.ed.gov/programs/digest/d13/tables/dt13_303.10.asp (accessed May 25, 2014).

9. "OECD Education at a Glance, 2013: OECD Indicators," Table A1.3a, Percentage of the population that has attained tertiary education by type of programme and age group (2011), OECD Publishing http://www.oecd.org/edu/eag2013%20(eng)--FINAL%2020%20June%202013.pdf (accessed May 27, 2014).

10. "U.S. Falls in Global Rankings of Young Adults Who Finish College," Daniel deVise, *The Washington Post*, September 13, 2011 http://dx.doiorg/10.1787/eag-2013-en.

11. "U.S. Attainment Rates, Demographics, and the Supply of College Graduates," Arthur M. Hauptman, *Change, The Magazine of Higher Learning*, May–June 2013.

12. "OECD Education at a Glance, 2013, Country Note, United States," http://www.oecd.org/edu/United%20States%20_EAG2013%20 Country%20Note.pdf (accessed May 25, 2014).

13. "A Stronger Nation Through Higher Education," The Lumina Foundation, June 2013, http://www.luminafoundation.org/ publications/A_stronger_nation_through_higher_education-2013. pdf (accessed May 27, 2014).

14. "Coming to Our Senses: Education and the American Future," report of the College' Board's Commission on Access, Admission and Success in Higher Education, 2008, https:// professionals.collegeboard.com/profdownload/coming-to-our-senses-college-board-2008.pdf (accessed May 27, 2014).

15. "College Board Hearts College Bubble," George Leef, The John William Pope Center for Higher Education Policy blog, November 20, 2013, http://www.popecenter.org/commentaries/article.html? id=2932#.U4JVAI1OWic (accessed May 25, 2014).

16. *Is College Worth It?*, by William J. Bennett with David Wilezol (Thomas Nelson Inc, 2013), argues that the danger of student debt and irrelevant education should make young people consider career training or particular colleges known for producing high-earning graduates.

17. Statistics on selectivity of colleges is from "Institutions' acceptance rates; number of applications, admissions, and enrollees; and enrollees' SAT and ACT scores, by control and level of institution: 2011–12," Digest of Education Statistics, Table 374, http://nces.ed.gov/programs/digest/d12/tables/ dt12_374.asp, (accessed May 27, 2014); statistic on enrollment at open-admissions institutions comes from "Trends in College Pricing 2013," The College Board, http://trends.collegeboard. org/sites/default/files/college-pricing-2013-full-report.pdf (accessed May 27, 2014).

18. "State of College Admission, 2013," Melissa E. Clinedinst, Sarah F. Hurley, and David A. Hawkins, National Association for

College Admission Counseling, 2014, available via http://www. nacacnet.org/research/PublicationsResources/Marketplace/ research/Pages/StateofCollegeAdmission.aspx (accessed May 27, 2014) and "The American Freshman, National Norms, Fall 2013."

19. "Class of 2018 Admit Rates Lowest in University History," Alex Zivkovic, *The Stanford Daily*, March 28, 2014.

20. "Institutions' acceptance rates; number of applications, admissions, and enrollees; and enrollees' SAT and ACT scores, by control and level of institution: 2011–12," Digest of Education Statistics, Table 374, http://nces.ed.gov/programs/digest/d12/ tables/dt12_374.asp (accessed May 25, 2014).

21. "Unequal Family Income and Unequal Educational Opportunity, 1970–2012," *Postsecondary Education Opportunity*, October, 2013.

22. In 1975, 63.7 percent of high-income students enrolled versus 34.7 percent of low-income students, per "Percentage of recent high school completers enrolled in 2-year and 4-year college, by income level, 1975 through 2011"; Digest of Education Statistics, Table 236, http://nces.ed.gov/programs/digest/d12/tables/dt12_236.asp (accessed May 25, 2014).

23. "Gains and Gaps: Changing Inequality in U.S. College Entry and Completion," Martha J. Bailey and Susan M. Dynarski, 2011, National Bureau of Economic Research Working Paper No. 17633, http://www.nber.org/papers/w17633 (accessed May 27, 2014).

24. The drop is based on analysis that looked at the distribution of bachelor's degrees awarded to students grouped by family-income quartiles; the analysis on degree completion examined bachelor's degree completion rates for dependent eighteen-to-twenty-four-year-olds from 1970 to 2011, from "Family Income and Unequal Educational Opportunity 1970–2011," Thomas G. Mortenson, *Postsecondary Education Opportunity*, November 2012.

25. "Merit Aid for Undergraduates, Trends from 1995–96 to 2007–08," a *Stats in Brief* report from the U.S. Department of Education,

Jenny H. Woo and Susan P. Choy, MPR Associates Inc., October 2011; these data looked only at full-time students attending college for the first time, http://nces.ed.gov/pubs2012/2012160.pdf (accessed May 27, 2014).

26. "Undermining Pell: How Colleges Compete for Wealthy Students and Leave the Low-Income Behind," Stephen Burd, New American Foundation, May 2013.

27. Among the most-cited of such studies is "Access Denied: Restoring the Nation's Commitment to Equal Educational Opportunity," a report by the federal Advisory Committee on Student Financial Assistance, February 2001, http://www2.ed.gov/about/bdscomm/list/acsfa/access_denied.pdf (accessed May 25, 2014).

28. "Undermining Pell," 2013.

29. "Undermining Pell," 2013.

30. "Merit Aid for Undergraduates," 2011.

31. Personal observations, January 2012.

32. Per the Food and Nutriton Service of the U.S. Department of Agriculture, Office of the Chief Communications Officer, March 28, 2014, response to the author's inquiry.

33. *Postsecondary Education Opportunity*, July 2013.

34. Pell Grant data on for-profit college student for 1980 drawn from "1980–81 Federal Pell Grant Program End-of-Year Report," by the U.S. Department of Education, issued in August 1982; data for 2011 drawn from *Postsecondary Education Opportunity*, July 2013.

35. Pell Grant data on for-profit college students for 2011 drawn from the 2011–12 Federal Pell Grant Program End-of-Year Report by Mary Mille at the U.S. Department of Education; data on community-college recipients are from *Postsecondary Education Opportunity*, July 2013.

36. "Separate and Unequal, How Higher Education Reinforces the Intergenerational Reproduction of White Racial Privilege," Anthony P. Carnevale and Jeffrey Strohl, Georgetown University

Center on Education and the Workforce, July 2013, https://george
town.app.box.com/s/zhi9ilgzba9ncmr16ral (accessed May 27, 2014).

37. "Separate and Unequal," 2013.

38. The Clearinghouse rate is higher than the rate of 12 percent,
based on the official federal formula for graduation rates, which
is often cited for this statistic. But the 12 percent figure does not
adequately capture the results of students who transfer, and
many experts are increasingly considering Clearinghouse estimates as more reliable.

39. "Bridging the Higher Education Divide: Strengthening
Community Colleges and Restoring the American Dream,"
Report of the Task Force, Century Foundation May 2013, http://
tcf.org/assets/downloads/20130523-Bridging_the_Higher_
Education_Divide-REPORT-ONLY.pdf (accessed May 27, 2014).

40. "Initial College Attendance of Low-Income Young Adults,"
Institute for Higher Education Policy, June 2011, http://www.
ihep.org/assets/files/publications/m-r/Portraits-
Low-Income_Young_Adults_Attendance_Brief_FINAL_
June_2011.pdf (accessed May 27, 2014).

41. According to the Department of Education's online College
Affordability and Transparency Center, average tuition at a community college was about $2,900 in fall 2011, versus about $14,000
at a two-year for-profit; dozens of the most expensive two-year
for-profits charge more than seven times as much as community
colleges.

42. "The For-Profit Postsecondary School Sector: Nimble Critters
or Agile Predators?" David J. Deming, Claudia Golden, and
Lawrence F. Katz, *Journal of Economic Perspectives*, 26(1), 139–164
winter 2012, available via http://scholar.harvard.edu/goldin/pub
lications/profit-postsecondary-school-sector-nimble-critters-or-
agile-predators (accessed May 27, 2014).

43. "Profiting Higher Education: What Students, Alumni and Employers Think About For-Profit Colleges," Carol Hagelskamp, David

Schleifer, and Christopher DiStasi, *Public Agenda*, February 2014, http://www.publicagenda.org/pages/profiting-higher-education (accessed May 7, 2014).

44. Author interview with Mark C. Long, January 14, 2014.

45. Author interview with Mark C. Long, January 14, 2014.

46. *Fisher v. University of Texas at Austin* (No. 11–345).

47. *Crossing the Finish Line: Completing College at America's Public Universities*, William G. Bowen, Matthew M. Chingos, and Michael S. McPherson, Princeton University Press, 2009.

48. "The Missing One-Offs: The Hidden Supply of High-Achieving Low-Income Students," Caroline Hoxby and Christopher Avery, Brookings Papers on Economic Activity, Spring 2013, http://www.brookings.edu/~/media/projects/bpea/spring%202013/2013a_hoxby.pdf (accessed May 25, 2014).

49. "The Missing One-Offs," 2013 (Note: Because college-going families have higher incomes than the population as a whole, the lowest quartile of family income is also higher than that of the overall population.)

50. *Top Student, Top School? How Social Class Shapes Where Valedictorians Go to College*, Alexandria Walton Radford, University of Chicago Press, 2013.

51. "The Missing One-Offs," 2013.

52. "Undermatch Is Underthought," Mark Schneider, blog post on *The Quick and the Ed.* January 7, 2014 (Cached copy accessed May 25, 2014, http://webcache.googleusercontent.com/search?q=cache:http://www.quickanded.com/2014/01/undermatch-is-underthought.html).

53. "The Condition of College & Career Readiness 2013 First Generation Students Report," ACT and Council for Opportunity in Education, November 4, 2013, http://www.act.org/newsroom/data/2013/states/pdf/FirstGeneration.pdf (accessed May 25, 2014).

54. "Remediation: Higher Education's Bridge to Nowhere," Complete College American, April, 2012, http://www.completecollege.org/docs/CCA-Remediation-final.pdf (accessed May 25, 2014).

55. "Bridge to Nowhere."

56. "Online Learning: Does It Help Low-Income and Underprepared Students?" Shanna Smith Jaggers, Community College Research Center Working Papers, January 2011, additional related research can be found at the center's web site, http://ccrc.tc.columbia.edu/Online-Education-Instructional-Technology.html (accessed May 25 2014).

57. "Home Broadband 2013," Kathryn Zickuhr and Aaron Smith, Pew Internet & American Life Project, August 3013, http://www.pewinternet.org/2013/08/26/home-broadband-2013/ (accessed May 27, 2014).

Part Two

1. "Education and Training," BMO Capital Markets, September 2013.

2. As it happens, 2011, the latest year for which these data are available, was a strong year for endowment returns; in 2008, a year of poor endowment returns, tuition accounted for about 29 percent of private research universities' revenues.

3. "Trends in College Spending, 2001–2011: Updated Charts and Tables," Delta Cost Project, American Institute for Research, pre-release copy reviewed by author was dated March 2014.

4. From data compiled by Moody's Investors Service for this book, 2014.

5. Cited in "Myths About College and University Endowments" fact sheet produced by Association of American Universities, quoting findings from the "2008 NACUBO Endowment Study," National Association of College and University Business Officers, January, 2009.

6. "2007 NACUBO Endowment Study," National Association of College and University Business Officers, January, 2008.

7. Figures on endowment values and returns are taken from various annual NACUBO Endowment Study reports in these periods.

8. Statement of Jane G. Gravelle of the Congressional Research Service, before the Committee on Finance, U.S. Senate, September 26, 2007, http://www.finance.senate.gov/imo/media/doc/092607testjg1.pdf (accessed May 27, 2014).

9. "Voluntary Support of Education, 2012," Ann E. Kaplan, Council for Aid to Education, 2013.

10. "Million Dollar Ready: Assessing the Institutional Factors that Lead to Transformational Gifts," Johnson Grossnickle & Associates and Lilly Family School of Philanthropy at Indiana University, December 2013, http://www.philanthropy.iupui.edu/files/research/million_dollar_ready_report_v3.pdf (accessed May 27, 2014).

11. "Trends in College Spending, 2001–2011."

12. Ibid.

13. From a table based on data from State Higher Education Executive Officers appearing in "An Era Neglect," *The Chronicle of Higher Education*, March, 3, 2014.

14. "Improving Postsecondary Education Through the Budget Process: Challenges & Opportunities," National Association of State Budget Officers, Spring 2013, http://www.nasbo.org/sites/default/files/pdf/Improving%20Postsecondary%20Education%20Through%20the%20Budget%20Process-Challenges%20and%20Opportunities.pdf (accessed May 27, 2014).

15. "Higher Education Finance FY 2013," State Higher Education Executive Officers, 2014, http://www.sheeo.org/resources/publications/shef-%E2%80%94-state-higher-education-finance-fy13 (accessed May 27, 2014).

16. Ibid.

17. "Recent Deep State Higher Education Cuts May Harm Students and the Economy for Years to Come," Center on Budget and Policy Priorities, March 19, 2013, http://www.cbpp.org/cms/?fa=view&id=3927 (accessed May 27, 2014).

18. Ibid.

19. "State Need-Based Grant Aid, 1979 to 2012," Thomas G. Mortenson, *Postsecondary Education Opportunity*, August 2013.

20. "43rd Annual Survey Report on State-Sponsored Student Financial Aid, 2011–2012 Academic Year," National Association of State Student Aid Grant Programs annual survey, available via http://www.nassgap.org/viewrepository.aspx?categoryID=351# document_936 (accessed May 27, 2014).

21. "State Disinvestment in Higher Education FY1961 to FY2013," Thomas G. Mortenson, *Postsecondary Education Opportunity*, February, 2013.

22. "Public Policies, Prices, and Productivity in American Higher Education," Arthur M. Hauptman, part of the Stretching the Higher Education Dollar series of published by American Enterprise Institute, April, 2013, http://www.aei.org/files/ 2013/04/11/-public-policies-prices-and-productivity-in-ame rican-higher-education_082108551799.pdf (accessed May 27, 2014).

23. *The Rising Costs of Higher Education: A Reference Handbook*, John R. Thelin, ABC-CLIO, 2013.

24. "College Costs Surge 500 percent in U.S. Since 1985: Chart of the Day," Bloomberg News, Michelle Jamrisko and Ilan Kolet, August 26, 2013.

25. *Why Does College Cost So Much?* Robert B. Archibald and David H. Feldman, Oxford University Press, 2011.

26. "Trends in College Pricing, 2013."

27. Ibid.

28. Ibid.

29. Author interview, April 2014; Van Buskirk's advice can be found at: bestcollegefit.com.

30. Based on an analysis of data from the U.S. Department of Education's National Postsecondary Student Aid Study, by Mark Kantrowitz for this book.

31. "Income Stratification of Undergraduate Enrollments by Level and Sector 1988 to 2011," Thomas G. Mortenson, *Postsecondary Education Opportunity*, July 2013.

32. "The Graduate Student Debt Review: The State of Graduate Student Borrowing," Jason Delisle, Policy Brief, New America Foundation, March 2014, http://newamerica.net/sites/newamerica.net/files/policydocs/GradStudentDebtReview-Delisle-Final.pdf (accessed May 27, 2014).

33. "Trends in Student Aid, 2013," The College Board, 2013, http://trends.collegeboard.org/sites/default/files/student-aid-2013-full-report.pdf (accessed May 27, 2014).

34. "Student Debt and the Class of 2012," The Project on Student Debt, December, 2013, http://projectonstudentdebt.org/files/pub/classof2012.pdf.

35. "Financial Aid 101: A Guide to Understanding Federal Financial Aid Programs for Community College Trustees and Leaders," Association of Community College Trustees, 2013, http://www.acct.org/files/Publications/ACCTFinAid101.pdf.

36. Based on a loan-payment calculator found at the web site, FinAid.org, assuming an average loan balance of $29,400 and a 6.21-percent interest rate for an unsubsidized. The calculation for a subsidized loan assumes a rate of 4.66 percent. The interest rates are those that went into effect in July 2014.

37. "Marketplace Money," July 5, 2013.

38. "Student Loans Are Widening the Wealth Gap: Time to Focus on Equity," Assets and Education Initiative, University of Kansas School of Social Welfare, 2013, http://save2limitdebt.com/wp-content/uploads/2013/11/Student-Loans-Widening-Wealth-Gap_Fullreport.pdf (accessed May 27, 2014).

39. "Loans for Educational Opportunity: Making Borrowing Work for Today's Students," Susan Dynarski and Daniel Kreisman, The Hamilton Project, Brookings Institution, 2013,

http://www.hamiltonproject.org/files/downloads_and_links/ THP_DynarskiDiscPaper_Final.pdf (accessed May 27, 2014).

40. The rate for unsubsidized and graduate loans was initially set at 5.41 percent with a 9.5 percent cap and those for PLUS loans, typically taken out by parents, at 6.41 percent with a 10.5 percent cap.

41. "Public Policies, Prices, and Productivity in American Higher Education."

42. Ibid.

43. *The Cost Disease: Why Computers Get Cheaper and Health Care Doesn't*, William J. Baumol with contributions from others, Yale University Press, 2012.

44. "Get Your College Education Here, Prices Slashed," Scott Carlson and Andy Thomason, *The Chronicle of Higher Education*, September 30, 2013.

45. "Enrollment: A Moving Target for Many Colleges," Scott Carlson, Goldie Blumenstyk, and Andy Thomason, *The Chronicle of Higher Education*, October 15, 2013.

46. "Private Distress," Ry Rivard, *Inside Higher Ed*, December 9, 2013.

47. "Program Cuts, Layoffs Coming to Iowa Wesleyan," B. A. Morelli. *The Gazette*, January 24, 2014.

48. "Certificates: Gateway to Gainful Employment and College Degrees," Anthony P. Carnevale, Stephen J. Rose, Andrew R. Hanson, Georgetown University Center on Education and the Workforce, June 2012, http://cew.georgetown.edu/certificates (accessed May 27, 2014).

49. Statistics on Pell Grants from the Department of Education's "2001–02 Title IV Federal Pell Grant End-of-Year Report" and the "2012–12 Federal Pell Grant Report;" data on military tuition assistance is from Exhibit 129 of BMO's "Education and Training," 2013; data on veterans education benefits from "With GI Bill's Billions at Stake, Colleges Compete to Lure Veterans," Libby Sander, *The Chronicle of Higher Education*, April 27, 2012.

50. Per author interview with university officials.

51. "Demography as Destiny: Policy Considerations in Enrollment Management," Policy Insights, Western Interstate Commission for Higher Education, April, 2013, http://www.wiche.edu/info/publications/PI-knocking2013.pdf (accessed May 27, 2014).

52. "Knight Commission Unveils College Sports Database," *USA Today,* December 4, 2013.

53. "Debt Loads Weigh Heavily on Athletics Programs," Brad Wolverton, *The Chronicle of Higher Education,* September 28, 2009.

54. Knight Commission on Intercollegiate Athletics, 2012.

55. Jeff Smith's unpublished paper, "Positioning Athletics Within the Academic Mission of Universities," provided to the author in January 2014.

56. "Intercollegiate Athletic Success and Donations at NCAA Division I Institutions," Brad R. Humphreys and Michael Mondello, *Journal of Sports Management,* 2007 21, 265–280, Human Kinetics Inc., 2007, http://www.ashe.ws/images/HumphreysMondello2007.pdf (accessed May 27, 2014).

57. "University Start-Ups: Critical for Improving Technology Transfer," Walter D. Valdivia, Center for Technology Innovation at Brookings, November 2013, http://www.brookings.edu/~/media/research/files/papers/2013/11/start%20ups%20tech%20transfer%20valdivia/valdivia_tech%20transfer_v29_no%20embargo.pdf (accessed May 27, 2014).

58. "Losing Focus: The Annual Report on the Economic Status of the Profession, 2013–14," American Association of University Professors, available via http://www.aaup.org/article/losing-focus-annual-report-economic-status-profession-2013-14#.U4TsQCjDWCk (accessed May 27, 2014).

59. "Here's the News: The Annual Report on the Economic Status of the Profession, 2012–2013" (and the 2011–12 report for the comparison to tuition), John W. Curtis and Saranna

Thornton, American Association of University Professors, available via http://www.aaup.org/report/heres-news-annual-report-economic-status-profession-2012-13 (accessed May 27, 2014).

60. "Losing Focus."

61. "Here's the News."

62. "Trends in College Spending, 1998 to 2008: Where Does the Money Come From/ Where Does It Go? What Does It Buy?" Donna M. Desrochers, Colleen M. Lenihan, and Jane V. Wellman, A Report of the Delta Cost Project, http://www.deltacostproject.org/sites/default/files/products/Trends-in-College-Spending-98-08.pdf (accessed May 27, 2014).

63. "20 Years Later, How One Flagship Has Changed," Goldie Blumenstyk, *The Chronicle of Higher Education*, December 12, 2008.

64. *The Fall of the Faculty: The Rise of the All-Administrative University and Why It Matters*, Benjamin Ginsberg, Oxford University Press, 2011.

65. "Administrative Bloat at American Universities: The Real Reason for High Costs in Higher Education," Jay P. Greene, Brian Kisida, and Jonathan Mills, Goldwater Institute Policy Report, August 17, 2010, http://goldwaterinstitute.org/sites/default/files/Administrative%20Bloat.pdf (accessed May 27, 2014).

66. "Baumol and Bowen Cost Effects in Research Universities," Robert E Martin and R. Carter Hill, October 2013. Available at SSRN: http://ssrn.com/abstract=2153122 (accessed May 27, 2014).

67. "Labor Intensive or Labor Expensive?: Changing Staffing and Compensation Patterns in Higher Education," Issue Brief, Donna M. Desrochers and Rita Kirshstein, Delta Cost Project, American Institutes for Research, February, 2014, http://www.deltacostproject.org/sites/default/files/products/DeltaCostAIR_Staffing_Brief_2_3_14.pdf (accessed May 27, 204).

68. "Employees in degree-granting institutions, by sex, employ-
    ment status, control and level of institution, and primary occu-
    pation: Selected years, fall 1991 through fall 2011," Digest of
    Education Statistics, 2012 Tables and Figures, Table 284, http://
    nces.ed.gov/programs/digest/d12/tables/dt12_284.asp (accessed
    May 27, 2014).

69. "College as Country Club: Do Colleges Cater to Students'
    Preferences for Consumption?" Brian Jacob, Brian McCall,
    and Kevin M. Stange, National Bureau of Economic Research
    Working Paper, No 18745, issued January 2013, http://www.nber.
    org/papers/w18745 (accessed May 27, 2014).

70. "The Financially Sustainable University," Jeff Denneen and Tom
    Dretler, Bain & Company and Sterling Partners, July 2012, avail-
    able via http://www.bain.com/publications/articles/financially-
    sustainable-university.aspx (accessed May 27, 2014).

71. "Rising Debt Engulfs Colleges as Well as Students," Don Troop,
    The Chronicle of Higher Education, August 26, 2013.

72. "How the Campus Crumbles: Colleges Face Challenges from
    Deferred Maintenance," Scott Carlson, *The Chronicle of Higher
    Education*, May 20, 2012, plus additional stories by Carlson.

Part Three

1. "Gallup–*Inside Higher Ed* College and University Presidents
   Panel—Inaugural Survey Findings, Presidents Bullish on Their
   Institutions, But Not on Massive Open Online Courses and
   Higher Education Generally," Gallup, May 2, 2013.

2. "Strong Leadership at Colleges Is Key as Flow of Dollars Ebbs,
   Moody's Analyst Says," Scott Carlson, *The Chronicle of Higher
   Education*, June 10, 2011.

3. "College Presidents Harbor Doubts About Governing Boards,"
   Ry Rivard, *Inside Higher Ed*, September 4, 2013.

4. "Statement in Response to President Obama's August 22, 2013 Speech at SUNY Buffalo," New Faculty Majority, 2013, http://academeblog.org/2013/08/29/the-new-faculty-majoritys-statement-in-response-to-president-obamas-august-22-2013-speech-at-suny-buffalo/ (accessed May 27, 2014).

5. "The Just-in-Time Professor" A Staff Report Summarizing eForum responses on the Working Conditions of Contingent Faculty in Higher Education, House Committee on Education and the Workforce Democratic Staff, U.S. House of Representatives, January 2014, http://www.mpsanet.org/Portals/0/1.24.14-AdjunctEforumReport.pdf (accessed May 27, 2014).

6. Ibid.

7. V.C. Smith, as cited in "Changing Faculty Workforce Models," Adrianna Kezar, TIAA-CREF Institute, https://www.tiaa-crefinstitute.org/public/pdf/changing-faculty-workforce-models.pdf (accessed May 27, 2014).

8. "The American College President, 2012" Brian Cook and Young Kim, American Council on Education, 2012 summarized in: http://www.acenet.edu/the-presidency/columns-and-features/Pages/The-American-College-President-Study.aspx (accessed May 27, 2014).

9. "New Chiefs of 2-Year Colleges Must Met Revenue and Innovation Challenges," Sara Lipka, *The Chronicle of Higher Education,* April 22, 2013.

10. Crisis and Opportunity: Aligning the Community College Presidency with Student Success," The Aspen Institute, 2013 http://www.aspeninstitute.org/sites/default/files/content/upload/CEP_Final_Report.pdf (accessed May 27, 2014).

11. "State Performance Funding for Higher Education: Silver Bullet or Red Herring?" David Tandberg and Nicholas Hillman, WISCAPE Policy Brief, University of Wisconsin-Madison, Wisconsin Center for the Advancement of Postsecondary Education, 2013,

http://www.wiscape.wisc.edu/docs/WebDispenser/wiscaped-ocuments/pb018.pdf?sfvrsn=4 (accessed May 27, 014).

12. *We're Losing Our Minds: Rethinking American Higher Education,* Richard P. Keeling and Richard H. Hersh, Palgrave Macmillan, 2011.

13. "A Test of Leadership: Charting the Future of U.S. Higher Education," The Commission Appointed by U.S. Secretary of Education Margaret Spellings, U.S. Department of Education, 2006 http://www2.ed.gov/about/bdscomm/list/hiedfuture/reports/pre-pub-report.pdf (accessed May 27, 2014).

14. "Knowing What Students Know and Can Do: The Current State of Student Learning Outcomes Assessment in U.S. Colleges and Universities," George D. Kuh, Natasha Jankowsi, Stanley O. Ikenberry, and Jillian Kinzie, National Institute for Learning Outcomes Assessment, January 2014, http://www.learningout comeassessment.org/documents/2013%20Survey%20Report%20 Final.pdf (accessed May 27, 2014).

15. "Have U.S. 'Shame Lists' Helped Lower Tuition? Probably Not," Kelly Field and Jonah Newman, *The Chronicle of Higher Education,* February 24, 2014.

16. "The Gates Effect," a series of articles in *The Chronicle of Higher Education,* various authors, July 14, 2013.

17. "'Advocacy Philanthropy' and the Public Policy Agenda: The Role of Modern Foundations in American Higher Education," Cassie Hall and Scott L. Thomas, April 2012, as quoted in *The Chronicle.*

18. "The Gates Effect" Marc Parry, Kelly Field, and Beckie Supiano, *The Chronicle of Higher Education,* July 14, 2013.

19. "By the Numbers: Millionaires at Private Colleges, 2011" Jonah Newman, *The Chronicle of Higher Education,* December 15, 2013.

20. "The Sallie Mae Saga: A Government-Created, Student Debt Fueled Profit Machine," Deanne Loonin, National Consumer Law Center, January 2014, http://www.studentloanborroweras

sistance.org/wp-content/uploads/File/report-sallie-mae-saga. pdf (accessed May 27, 2014).

21. "Boom—Bust—Boom: Deal Velocity" courtesy of GSV Advisors, 2014.

Part Four

1. "Disrupting College: How Disruptive Innovation Can Deliver Quality and Affordability to Postsecondary Education," Clayton M. Christensen, Michael B. Horn, Louis Caldera, and Louis Soares, Center for American Progress and Innosight Institute, February 2011, http://www.americanprogress.org/wp-content/ uploads/issues/2011/02/pdf/disrupting_college.pdf (accessed May 27, 2014).

2. "Faculty Backlash Grows Against Online Partnerships," Steve Kolowich, *The Chronicle of Higher Education*, May 10, 2013.

3. *Beyond the MOOC Hype: A Guide to Higher Education's High Tech Disruption*, Jeffrey R. Young, Kindle edition, 2013.

4. "Getting to the Bottom of the $10,000 Bachelor's Degree," Eric Kelderman, *The Chronicle of Higher Education*, March 4, 2013.

5. Ibid.

6. *Why Public Higher Education Should Be Free: How to Decrease Cost and Increase Quality at American Universities*, Robert Samuels, Rutgers University Press, 2013; other proposals include "Redefining College Affordability: Securing America's Future With a Free Two-Year College Option Opportunity," Sara Goldrick-Rab and Nancy Kendall, prepared under the auspices of The Education Optimists, for the Lumina Foundation, April, 2014, http://www.luminafoundation.org/publications/ideas_ summit/Redefining_College_Affordability.pdf (accessed June 5, 2014) and proposals from Redeeming America's Promise, released June 2014, http://www.redeemingamericaspromise. org/ (accessed June 5, 2014).

7. Interview with the author, February 3, 2014.

8. *College UnBound: The Future of Higher Education and What It Means for Students*, Jeffrey J. Selingo, New Harvest, Hougton Mifflin Harcourt, 2013.

9. "Training for Success: A Policy to Expand Apprenticeship in the United States," Ben Olinsky and Sarah Ayres, Center for American Progress, December 2013, http://www.americanprogress.org/wp-content/uploads/2013/11/apprenticeship_report.pdf (accessed May 27, 2014).

10. "Are We Losing Our Liberal Arts Colleges?" David W. Breneman, originally published by *The College Board Review*, No. 156, Summer 1990 and "Where Are They Now? Revisiting Breneman's Study of Liberal Arts Colleges," Vicki L. Baker, Roger G. Baldwin, and Sumedha Makker, *Liberal Education*, Association of American Colleges and Universities, Volume 98, No. 3, Summer 2012, http://www.aacu.org/liberaleducation/le-su12/baker_baldwin_makker.cfm (accessed May 27, 2014).

11. "Saving the Life of the Mind: As Pressure Mounts to Produce Skilled Workers, Colleges Try to Promote Intellectual Values," Goldie Blumenstyk, *The Chronicle of Higher Education*, February 28, 2010.

12. "How Liberal Arts and Science Majors Fare in Employment," Debra Humphreys and Patrick Kelly, National Center for Higher Education Management Systems and Association of American Colleges and Universities, January 2014, available via http://www.aacu.org/leap/nchems/ (accessed May 27, 2014).

13. "Standing in the Light: Release of U.S. Federal Data Means Online Learning Has Really Arrived," blog post by Richard Garrett, The Observatory on Borderless Higher Education, January 13, 2014. available via http://www.obhe.ac.uk/documents/view_details?id=949 (accessed May 27, 2014).

14. "Conflicted: Faculty and Online Education, 2012," A joint project of the Babson Survey Research Group and *Inside Higher Ed*, Elaine Allen, Jeff Seaman, Doug Lederman, and Scott Jaschik, June 2012, http://www.insidehighered.com/sites/default/server_files/files/IHE-BSRG-Conflict.pdf (accessed May 7, 2014).

FURTHER READING

News Media

The Chronicle of Higher Education

The Hechinger Report

Inside Higher Ed

General Information on Higher Education

American Educational Research Association

Center on Higher Education Reform at American Enterprise Institute

Education Sector at the American Institutes for Research Quick & the Ed blog

The Education Trust

The Hamilton Project at the Brookings Institution

The Lumina Foundation

The New America Foundation

Student and Demographic Issues

Cooperative Institutional Research Program, Higher Education Research Institute, at University of California at Los Angeles

Institute for Higher Education

Pell Institute for the Study of Opportunity in Higher Education

The Century Foundation

Western Interstate Commission on Higher Education

For-Profit Colleges

Center for Analysis of Postsecondary Education and Employment

"The Harkin Report," the informal name for the United States Senate Health Education, Labor and Pensions Committee report: "For Profit Higher Education: The Failure to Safeguard the Federal Investment and Ensure Student Success," July 30, 2012, plus profiles of 30 companies, all available via http://www.harkin.senate.gov/help/forprofitcolleges.cfm

Colleges Costs

Delta Cost Project at the American Institutes of Research

Knight Commission on Intercollegiate Athletics

State Higher Education Executive Officers

The College Board

Student Debt

National Consumer Law Center

Project on Student Debt at The Institute for College Access & Success

Young Invincibles

The Economic Payoffs from Higher Education

Center on Education and the Workforce, Georgetown University,

College Measures

Disruption and Innovation in Higher Education

Center for American Progress

Clayton Christensen Institute

Creative Commons (for information on open educational resources)

Open Learning Initiative at Carnegie Mellon University

The Saylor Foundation

WICHE Cooperative for Educational Technologies (WCET)

Works Cited or Otherwise Consulted for this Book

Academically Adrift: Limited Learning on College Campuses, Richard Arum and Josipa Roksa, University of Chicago Press, 2011.

Beyond the MOOC Hype: A Guide to Higher Education's High Tech Disruption, Jeffrey R. Young, Kindle edition, 2013.

The College Solution: The Guide for Everyone Looking for the Right School at the Right Price (Second Edition), Lynn O'Shaughnessy, FT Press, 2012.

College (Un)Bound: The Future of Higher Education and What It Means for Students, Jeffrey J. Selingo, New Harvest Houghton Mifflin Harcourt, 2013.

College: What It Was, Is, and Should Be, Andrew Delanco, Princeton University Press, 2012.

The Cost Disease: Why Computers Get Cheaper and Health Care Doesn't, William J. Baumol, (with contributions from others), Yale University Press, 2012.

Crossing the Finish Line: Completing College at America's Public Universities, William G. Bowen, Matthew M. Chingos, and Michael S. McPherson, Princeton University Press, 2009.

DIY U: Edupunks, Edupreneurs, and the Coming Transformation of Higher Education, Anya Kamenetz, Chelsea Green Publishing, 2010.

The Innovative University: Changing the DNA of Higher Education from the Inside Out, Clayton M. Christensen and Henry J. Eyring, Wiley, 2011.

The Fall of the Faculty: The Rise of the All-Administrative University and Why It Matters, Benjamin Ginsberg, Oxford University Press, 2011.

Higher Education?: How Colleges Are Wasting Our Money and Failing Our Kids—and What We Can Do About It, Andrew Hacker and Claudia Dreyfus, Times Books, 2010.

Is College Worth It?, William J. Bennett with David Wilezol, Thomas Nelson Inc., 2013.

The New Depression in Higher Education: A Study of Financial Aid Conditions at 41 Colleges and Universities, Earl F. Cheit, McGraw-Hill Book Company, 1971.

The Overeducated American, Richard B. Freeman, Academic Press, 1976.

The Rising Costs of Higher Education: A Reference Handbook, John R. Thelin, ABC-CLIO, 2013.

Top Student, Top School? How Social Class Shapes Where Valedictorians Go to College, Alexandria Walton Radford, University of Chicago Press, 2013.

Why Does College Cost So Much? Robert B. Archibald and David H. Feldman, Oxford University Press, 2011.

Why Public Higher Education Should Be Free: How to Decrease Cost and Increase Quality at American Universities, Robert Samuels, Rutgers University Press, 2013.

INDEX